Animals of Silence

IDRIS PARRY

Animals of Silence

Essays on Art, Nature, and Folk-tale

LONDON
OXFORD UNIVERSITY PRESS
1972

Oxford University Press, Ely House, London W1

GLASGOW NEW YORK TORONTO MELBOURNE WELLINGTON
CAPE TOWN IBADAN NAIROBI DAR ES SALAAM LUSAKA ADDIS ABABA
DELHI BOMBAY CALCUTTA MADRAS KARACHI LAHORE DACCA
KUALA LUMPUR SINGAPORE HONG KONG TOKYO

ISBN 0 19 212555 9

Printed in Great Britain by
The Camelot Press Ltd, London and Southampton

for
Eirwen

Contents

These essays, with the exception of 'The Dilemma of Lord Chandos', are revised versions of talks given on BBC Radio 3.

The Listener published the original broadcast text of 'Kafka, Rilke, and Rumpelstiltskin', 'The Druid and the Wren', 'Foam on the Wave', and 'Cordelia and the Button'. The broadcast version of 'The Tree of Movement' has appeared in *Language and Style* (Southern Illinois University).

German translations by Alfred Andersch of 'Cordelia and the Button' and 'Animals of Silence' have been published in the literary supplement of the *Neue Zürcher Zeitung*.

Everything that is, everything in the world that has form, whatever it may be, is a product of some force, a vestige of some energy and a symptom of some activity. In this sense, everything has been made....

ORTEGA Y GASSET

Kafka, Rilke, and Rumpelstiltskin

THE story of Rumpelstiltskin seems to have no relevance to the modern world, since it excludes the idea of mediocrity. There's no twilight in it, only choice between darkness of death and brilliance of glory. This girl who claims she can spin straw into gold knows that if she succeeds she can become a queen, but if she fails she will have her head chopped off. And who on earth can spin straw into gold? But this is not a story about the earth alone, it is a story about earth and heaven . . . or hell.

The girl is of this earth. She is like all of us, she wants glory beyond her obvious deserts; but she also realizes that to get beyond the obvious she must perform better than she knows. Of course she can't spin straw into gold, but if this is the only way to glory she will reach beyond her reach, and she does so, with the help of a strange little man who suddenly appears in her locked room. He is not human, he can do this task beyond human capabilities, he can spin straw into gold. He is both repulsive and attractive. His promise is exciting, his terms dangerous. He can make her a queen, and he does; but on one condition—she must give him the first child of her marriage.

The fool and the hero are not checked by doubt. They do not stop to think. For them there is neither conjecture nor qualification. This girl may be a fool, or possibly heroic; only her destiny can give the answer. She is now a queen. She has reached beyond her reach, but when the child comes she is content with the obvious. She does not wish to give the child away, she clings to human happiness and rejects the claim of that inhuman because superhuman monster. In her original state of misery it was easy to deny human limitations on any terms, but happiness has changed all that. Now human limitations are satisfactory, she is content, she wants her present bliss to last for ever, circumscribed, secure. She will not part with her child. Such a sacrifice seems to her an absurdity, and she forgets it is an exchange for a service equally absurd in human terms—the spinning of straw into gold.

The creature who can spin straw into gold is clearly more powerful than any human. He can destroy her. And yet, for a monster, he is really rather decent, since he gives her another chance to save herself by saving her child. He tells her he will let her off, he will release her from the bargain, but again on one condition—she must guess his name. This seems a lot easier than spinning straw into gold. But is it? Where is there certainty in confusion? He gives her another chance because in every moment there is a multitude of possibilities, and the additional chance is an additional opportunity to fall into perplexity. There is, of course, again the possibility of glory, but he is confident the odds are heavily against this. Now she is on her own, without his help, entirely human.

She soon finds that to strike on exactly the right name is beyond her conscious efforts. No word within her experience fits him. The task begins to look as absurdly impossible as the service she accepted and the promise she now denies. Is the face of the world always to be like this? And then the name is found. She finds it when she is not trying. It happens. By chance. As if by magic. Or is this discovery absurd too? When she is in the very pit of despair she is told the little man has been seen in the woods, singing out (most conveniently) that his name is Rumpelstiltskin. She is now the master. She plays with him, she pretends ignorance when they meet for the last time. She stumbles through a series of false guesses which raise him to an ecstasy of excitement as his prize seems to come nearer and nearer. Then she tells him his name, the real name, the only name. It's a lightning flash. In a fit of anger which might almost be called extravagant he grabs his left foot with both hands and tears himself apart. In this game it is all or nothing. He finds death, she gets glory. It could have been the other way round.

'Nimmy nimmy not, my name's Tom Tit Tot!' There are versions of 'Rumpelstiltskin' in so many countries that we may suspect it tells of deeply sensed truth. The story varies in detail from country to country, but the task is always humanly impossible. How then can the story be true? There is undoubtedly satisfaction for everybody in the achievement, since we must all hope to get more than we deserve and to perform better than we know. But doesn't this place the story firmly in the realm of fantasy? And yet, and yet . . . don't we secretly believe it is possible for footman to become king and for Cinderella, that nursery phoenix, to rise from the ashes and be transformed into glory? Belief in absurdity has another face, which is disbelief in the absurdity which is human life.

Whatever the variations in the story, there is always this insistent quest for the right name, an odd name, suddenly found and plucked out of darkness to bring power and release and happiness. The fundamental question is whether the discovery of the right name is an accident, unrelated to merit. If it is, then the whole thing is a swindle, and we should have every sympathy with that unfortunate monster. Can it be just coincidence that the little man gives his name away at precisely the right moment? Yes, it can—in the sense in which 'coincidence' means the falling together of events. There is a relationship which is not immediately apparent in the story, as it is never immediately apparent in life.

The word 'coincidence' for this concealed relationship is used by Franz Kafka in one of the conversations recorded by his young friend Gustav Janouch in Prague. 'Accident', said Kafka, 'is the name we give to a coincidence of events whose causation we do not know. But there is no world without causes. Therefore accidents do not really exist in the world, but only here . . .' And Kafka touched his head, then went on: 'There are accidents only in our heads, in our limited perceptions. They reflect the boundaries of our knowledge. The struggle against accident is always a struggle against ourselves, which we can never quite win.'

The limits of our knowledge are the concern of both science and art, which try to extend experience on the basis of what we know. This is why art too must be precise and objective. 'He was a poet', says Rilke, 'and he hated the approximate.' There is a right word for everything, a right name.

Rilke is haunted by the idea of limitation. In his essay 'Primal Sound' he talks about what he calls 'the five-fingered hand of the senses'. That is, each of our five senses is like a finger covering a certain sector of experience. What guarantee is there that the five senses together cover the whole of possible experience? There are gaps between our fingers; there are gaps between our senses. In these gaps is the darkness which hides the connections between events, the causation we cannot see. It is as if we live in a pool of light, so bright that the darkness beyond is intense. This darkness is the source of our vague fears, but also the home of the gods. They alone see the connections, the total relevance of everything that happens, that which now comes to us in bits and pieces, the 'accidents' which exist only in our heads, in our limited perceptions.

We do not know what the gods can see, and we want to know. In that perfect world of the gods, where all connections are visible, there can be no separation of the senses, no gaps, because experience is total. Rilke deliberately tries to mingle the senses, to fuse them, to establish a total sense-perception which is not divisible into five or any number. Harmony is indivisible, and Rilke's ultimate image of harmony is Orpheus.

Orpheus is both singer and hearer, the magic god who sings to nature and is, in his death, scattered over the earth to be the hearer of his own song. As both singer and hearer in one he forms a completed cycle. This ideal union of the senses is something Rilke tries to achieve here and now. The visible is heard, and in one poem music becomes 'audible landscape'. In another, written almost at the end of his life, Rilke is explicit:

> Somewhere music *stands*, as somewhere
> this light falls on ears as distant sound . . .
> Only to our senses does this seem separate.

So it is not surprising that Rilke often speaks of the poet's task as an activity on the frontier. And we find in Kafka's diaries a reference to his own writings as 'an assault on the frontier'; later he speaks of 'the constantly shifting frontier which lies between ordinary life and the terror which seems more real'.

Artists are fools. They think they can achieve the impossible. That girl is a fool too, when she says she can spin straw into gold. She knows it is impossible. The evidence of her senses tells her that. But the little man who comes from the dark and offers to help? Isn't he the faith which pushes beyond reason, beyond human evidence? He comes from the region outside the frontier of knowledge, the unknown with its wild fears and equally wild hopes. He is our dual image of the gods presented in one form; he is devilish in his darkness but divine in his promises. He represents a state of mind, the creative principle unchecked by rational doubt. He is the dangerous but vitally necessary adventure.

According to Mark Twain there is no laughter in heaven. If this is so, the little man must come from another place. She asks him to spin straw into gold, and he laughs. He can't stop laughing. Because, where he comes from, there is nothing in it. There, in that dark world where all connections are seen, not one thing is separate from another. To us, straw and gold stand opposite each other, opposite in the way Eve found herself opposite Adam at the dawn of consciousness, the beginning of fragmentation. The little man is still in Paradise. He has not eaten the poisoned apple and caught the plague of imperfection. He knows that, where all is one, straw is gold and gold is straw. That is why he laughs. This desperate girl is ready to pay him with her most precious possession for doing a job that needs no effort at all, since it is already done. Of course he agrees. She will pay, and is bound to pay, unless she discovers his name.

It is this 'unless' which makes the story. Now there is a possibility of change. The 'unless' introduces suspense and affirms the presence of life, because the one certain thing about any living substance is its constant uncertainty. One thing so easily becomes another. There is nothing so pleasing in the theatre as a sudden change of fortune—*peripeteia*. The fact that we have a technical term for it shows that it is convention, more than mere possibility. We can seldom explain it, but we always enjoy it, since it might happen to us. The downtrodden hero suddenly triumphs, poverty changes to wealth, misery to joy.

This is equivalent, in the world of Rumpelstiltskin, to the apparent change from straw to gold. The irrational event which is accepted as a natural possibility, the 'accident' which not only can happen but must happen of necessity, if only we are patient enough and wait long enough. The development is there, in the dark, and now the accidental is seen as a relevant part of total experience, where opposites coalesce. *Peripeteia* acknowledges that extremes proceed from a common source; it is only to our limited human perceptions that these are extremes and that there is such a state as being 'opposite'.

At the end of the story the girl's fortunes are suddenly transformed. Instead of being victim, she is now executioner. She knows in her flesh what it means to change from straw into gold, and the correspondence of outer and inner is complete. In human terms her good luck seems arbitrary, the result of mere chance, and we may wonder if it is altogether fair that she can sell her soul and keep it too. Just when the nameless stranger is jigging with delight at the prospect of taking possession of his prize, she fulfils his condition and strikes him to ashes. She names his name and conquers.

Naming the magic name is to exert power over nature. This woman not only has the last word; she has the only word, in the circumstances. Only one word will do now, but that one word is all-powerful. Gods, ghosts, and mortals: all could be harmed, according to the beliefs of primitive society, if their names were exposed. That is, pronounced, or even known. Primitive taboos on the utterance of certain names acknowledge belief that the essence of a person can be present in his name. To have power over the name is to have power over the person named. Language is concrete, and the name can conjure up object as well as person. That this belief still survives, even if consciously denied, is suggested by the prevalence of euphemism.

We damp our language down, perhaps for fear it may light up the dark. Society knows, and the taboos show it has known for a long time, that truth can be accurately projected in language. The existence of euphemism tells us that linguistic accuracy may be too sharp for comfort and that words have real power. Modifications are made, dangerous outlines blurred. Words become soft and friendly and dead, killed by the pleasant ease of habit. Euphemism is defensive indifference. It sacrifices form to good form. To know in advance the right thing to say on any occasion is infallibly to say the wrong thing. The right word emerges with a recognizable shock, brilliant from the dark. No poet has patience with the approximate.

To know the right name is to have power; to have the illusion of knowing the right name is to have the illusion of power. We may not wish to probe the dark; the right name may be too much for us, but no name at all is even more disturbing. When Macbeth stumbles across those secret, black, and midnight hags and asks them what they are doing, the answer he gets is: 'A deed without a name.' Nothing could be more terrible. As long as a deed remains without a name, its possibilities are boundless. It must be mastered before it masters us. It must be confined and known; that is, named. We cannot live without at least the illusion of control. We are not happy without names; even our abstractions must be made tangible in words.

B

Something must be said, a name must be uttered. We fear the unnamed as we fear the unknown. This is Rumpelstiltskin up to the last moment which brings the change. As long as he is unnamed he is the romantic principle, a confusion of boundless possibilities. He is passion, which can both destroy and create; there are fires in hell as well as in the life-giving sun. Destruction or creation, death or life—this is the choice before our heroine as she puzzles over the hidden name of her tormentor/benefactor. Only the name can resolve these apparent opposites. 'All things can be put into words,' says Kafka. In him, as in that girl, faith runs hand in hand with despair. He means that all things must be put into words. And he goes on to remind us of the phoenix, the combiner of opposites, the magic bird of passion destroyed in the fire to rise rejuvenated from the flames. 'All one's ideas, even the strangest, find a great fire ready for them, in which they are consumed and reborn.'

The girl goes through the great fire. She is consumed and reborn. She discovers the name. But what does she do to deserve knowledge? Nothing. It comes to her, she does not go to it; and she succeeds for this very reason. 'Stay at your table and listen,' says Kafka in one of his notebooks. 'Don't even listen, just wait, be completely quiet and alone. The world will offer itself to you to be unmasked. It cannot do otherwise. It will writhe before you in raptures.' This is what is offered to the girl. Rumpelstiltskin is the region beyond immediate experience. He writhes before her in raptures. The world of the unknown is always there, always waiting to be unmasked. It can be unmasked if it is given form, if the hidden connections are established. They are established when she names the name. She fulfils Kafka's condition, she waits, and the name is brought to her. Conscious effort is not enough, since it must stop at the frontier of consciousness.

She waits, and Rumpelstiltskin sings his name to her, through her friend. Strange coincidence. But there are no accidents. The theme of this story is man's return to the world of harmony, not through struggle against chance but by accepting chance as the necessity it must be in the world of total experience, where everything is integrated. 'He who does not seek will be found,' says Kafka. All the missing names are to be found beyond the frontier, in that area which is dark because unexplored. The name is the man, and Rumpelstiltskin is his name. And the name which is the man writhes before the girl in raptures because it cannot do otherwise. It is there to be discovered, uncovered. When Rumpelstiltskin surrenders his name he surrenders himself.

Giving form, establishing connections, naming the magic name—what is this but the fundamental business of art? 'Vision', says Jonathan Swift, 'is the art of seeing things invisible.' The connections are there, invisible. To find them, to name the magic name, is to sing the song of Orpheus and exert power over nature. Such a task has never been easy, this side of Paradise. Contradictions are almost friendly features of our landscape, and we can scarcely expect to see eternity every night. Yet the uncovering of the name which resolves contradictions is not merely possible (this would imply accident), it is inevitable. The name is there, to be found and uttered. Again Kafka defies despair with optimistic affirmation: 'It is certainly conceivable that the splendour of life in all its fullness lies in wait about everybody, but veiled and deep down, invisible, far away. But it lies there, not hostile, not reluctant, not deaf. If it is summoned by the right word, the right name, it will come. This is the essence of magic, which does not create but summons.'

Fairy-tales are for children, but also for everybody who senses that the world of logic has an open side, turned away from us. Is it possible we are not yet tuned to receive all that the world can say? Man sets up images of his gods and finds truth in the image, truth beyond immediate comprehension. Kafka speaks of his writings as a form of prayer. He is making his images of the gods.

Footpath on the Water

My house in Wales lies on the slope between sea and hills. When I go out and turn left at the gate I am soon on the path which takes me to the top. Here, from the centre of a horse-shoe of hills, I look down at the distant village. Houses among the trees, then a strip of sandy beach, the wide sea in front; and up here a mountain ridge curving away on either side, two arms which enclose the village and end in headlands which drop sharply into the water.

In the old days this view from the hills must have been the traveller's first sight of the village. He came this way. Those two headlands were impassable obstacles. Road and railway have been tunnelled through now and the approach is easy, but before the tunnels were made this descent from the hills was the only way. The traveller couldn't walk on the water. He looked for safety, so he made and followed these mountain paths, away from the cliffs and the sea and danger.

I like to follow these paths too. They are mute evidence, really and physically an imprint of man's endeavour. Nobody knows how old they are. The Romans came this way; their road from Canovium to Segontium runs a bit further inland. But these tracks are older than the Roman road. One of them touches the edge of a prehistoric circle of standing stones, where an archaeologist friend of mine dug an exploratory trench some years ago. He found evidence that the path was already there when the stones were erected. Granite is our rock, and it is known that neolithic axes were made here.

These tracks above the sea were trodden by the earliest travellers to and from Ireland. Medieval carts have left their ruts in the hardened soil. When I walk up there it is impossible not to speculate about the people who have been this way before.

It must have been this fascination of footpaths which aroused my interest in a special feature of Goethe's novel *Elective Affinities*, a book which is laced with footpaths. Goethe uses them, manipulates them, as a commentary on human behaviour, and in this story the symbolism of footpaths is closely linked to the symbolism of water. Footpaths and water—an association I find so familiar from my walks on those mountain tracks in sight of the sea.

In Goethe's novel we find an acceptable interchange between characters, but also an unusual emphasis on outer events which seem to have no direct connection with the human theme. The correspondence between the two features soon becomes clear. Goethe is providing an outer accompaniment to the inner action. The novel is always an outer accompaniment, and it is only here, on the surface, that thought is made visible and the unthinkable made plain.

The outer events begin as the progressive arrangement of a country estate. We follow its development. A relatively wild area of wooded hills is shaped into a planned paradise of footpaths and controlled water, each path, each pond, each bridge calculated for human convenience and pleasure. The owners of this estate, husband and wife, are presented at the outset as active, generous, civilized. Both have been married before. We find them directing the *arrangement* of their park to correspond to the *arrangement* of their lives (Goethe uses the same word for both). This marriage means control. It seems that the wilder aspects of human nature have been mastered in this couple, Charlotte and Eduard, as nature itself is now being mastered and civilized in the park.

But things do not go as planned. Control means there is something which must be controlled, and the impulse to freedom is not easily suppressed, in nature or in man. Eduard has been spoilt in earlier life. He is used to having his own way; and this is ominous. For an individual to have his own way is like giving absolute freedom to nature—the result can be intolerable to society. That classical restraint which is the arrangement of their lives when the book opens, has been won through effort and renunciation. Eduard now falls in love with a young girl, he abandons all restraint, he rushes off the footpath of human discipline in pursuit of her.

In this context, 'footpath' is no mere figure of speech, except as in literature speech is the word, which is real, the thing itself. Here the word is a fixed equivalent of fluid experience, the physical embodiment of an inner state; and the inner state is passion. Eduard does not yet know his inner state, he discovers it through action which draws on the unconscious as well as the conscious. It is action which makes the outer event, and this event then reveals to him, as well as to us, an impulse concealed up to now.

The impermissible takes shape. Goethe's equivalent is an overgrown footpath, familiar to Eduard (significantly enough) from his hunting trips. He leads the girl, Ottilie, along this path in search of an old mill. He does indeed leave the recognized, the civilized route: the path has been so little used in recent times that it soon peters out. They are lost among dark trees. The carefully-managed park has suddenly become jungle. Moss-covered rocks lie in the undergrowth. They hear water in the mill-wheel far below and make for the sound, familiar safety, but they have to climb down over dangerous rocks. Here there is no path. The romantic image is unmistakable.

Another event, seemingly independent of the inner action, coincides with the second stage in the crisis, Eduard's open declaration of love for Ottilie. It is not an exact coincidence in time. This event comes just before he declares his love, as their adventure on the overgrown footpath comes just before he realizes the existence of his passion. Art is the action which precedes consciousness and reveals the unknown; it is like an echo which comes to us before we know its origin and which then leads us to know that origin. So this event precedes and echoes Eduard's conscious act.

The event itself is connected with water. It is also related more obviously than that overgrown footpath to the well-being of society. Eduard, in his new extravagance of feeling, makes absurdly elaborate preparations to celebrate Ottilie's birthday. He organizes a house-party, and the public are invited into the park one evening to see a firework display, due to start after nightfall.

These landowners, as part of their programme to restrain and control nature, have converted three ponds into one ornamental lake, held at the lower end by a newly-built dam. Here, on the dam, the crowd gathers and grows, to watch the fireworks over the water. These jostling individuals, careless of each other's safety, like independent romantic particles, push forward impetuously, each trying to get a better place at the expense of his neighbour. There is no co-operation here, no discipline. The mob is passion. And this image of romantic dissolution develops further when a scream rises from the crowd—an uncivilized sound from an un-civilized centre. The dam has begun to break under the weight of people. It seems that the result of so much human effort is about to be destroyed, by passion. People in front fall into the lake and are in danger of drowning. The water which seemed so tame is suddenly hostile, a threat to human existence. But it was human action which made this water seem tame; it is human action which now makes it seem hostile.

The disaster is not complete. Only the fringe of the dam has collapsed. This is a warning, not the catastrophe itself. Those who have fallen in are rescued. One hovers between life and death, but he is soon restored. Human discipline saves the day, in the form of a heroic swimmer who organizes rescue and thinks only of others, not of himself.

This disturbing event drives the house-party indoors and Charlotte urges that the celebrations be abandoned. But

Eduard stays by the lake with Ottilie. He is not a heroic swimmer, he cares nothing for others. For him there is only his own insistent and particular desire. He now openly declares his love. He orders the servants to let off the fireworks, for them alone. He need hardly have said this: he has already let them off. The image of fire is a natural companion to those images of undisciplined crowd and uncontrolled water which have represented his state of mind for us.

Eduard cannot hide his feelings from his wife. Ottilie lives in the house with them. To forestall Charlotte's plan to send her away, Eduard himself leaves—and disappears from the story for a while. Ottilie remains. She is tortured by secret longings and a sense of guilt, deepened when Charlotte now gives birth to Eduard's child.

When Eduard returns, some months later, he comes without warning, secretly, stealthily, and keeps clear of the house. His conduct is typical: he lies in wait for the girl in the park, in ambush like an animal. He surprises her one evening when she is out for her usual walk with Charlotte's baby.

Footpaths and water—the same images recur, but this time in combination. He finds her by the lake, at the place where he declared his love. We are told he is driven there by irresistible impatience and that he makes his way deviously by paths known only to hunters and fishermen. Ottilie urges him to go away again. She loves him, but she also respects his marriage, which stands for the *arrangement* of society, for discipline and moral duty. She cannot shrug off her obligations as easily as he.

The hero of Goethe's earlier novel *The Sorrows of Young Werther* says there are two opposed inclinations in man. Either he surrenders willingly to restrictions and habit, or he strives for absolute experience and freedom. The choice is between the security of the known and the danger of the apparently limitless unknown. But even Werther, that hopeless romantic, notices that in this world it is seldom a plain case of either/or. There are many positions between the two extremes, positions which shade into one another. There must be, if life is to continue. The extremes themselves, these poles of classical discipline and romantic dissolution, of static and of fluid, are equally inimical to life.

Eduard knows nothing of the positions in between. There is no balance in this man. He is dominated by a single impulse, and there can be no balance where there is only one force. He is an extreme case, the unpleasant exaggeration which is equivalent to disease, and he infects Ottilie with his sickness. But he agrees to go when she pleads with him. He is influenced by her momentary moral determination. It is only momentary because she is also influenced by him. The seeds of dissolution are in all of us. She wavers, and the reversal follows. She is in his arms, she yields to that extreme of passion which is in her too, restrained up to now by her moral code but suddenly released by his touch like water from a dam which is really broken. For the first time she kisses him wildly, utterly without restraint. It is this which makes the decisive event, the echo which now, as the final revelation of corruption, follows the human act.

Eduard does go. Ottilie is left alone by the lake. It is already dark, she has the baby on her arm. Her mind is confused. Is it possible that by the house across the lake she can see a gleam from the white dress of Eduard's wife, who waits and wonders? She decides . . . But she doesn't decide; what happens now is a physical expression of her inner confusion. She is driven, in spite of herself, to take a shortcut across the water. It would take too long to go by her usual and recognized path, the safe path on land. She fears the water as she fears her passion, but she is driven into the boat by the impatience of despair. The inevitable happens. She is unable to control herself, so she is unable to control the boat. Spiritual distraction becomes physical. Panic is the ultimate collapse of reflective balance. The baby falls into the lake and is drowned.

The novel continues to the death of both Eduard and Ottilie, but the end is already here in the water, for her guilt cannot

outface this calamity. Later she speaks of her conduct in general
and says: 'I strayed from my path.' This could be applied
literally to her movements that night, but she means she has
strayed from the path of righteousness, which is her moral
code, security. For she adds, as if this were an obvious corollary:
'I broke my laws.'

So the path is the law, and the law is the path. But is there
law in free nature? Apparently not, in this conception. Goethe
has however already spoken in the novel about a different
human approach to natural force. Within the framework
of the book there is a short story (with other protagonists)
which makes explicit what has been implied in that earlier
incident of the heroic swimmer at the dam. And again it is
water which is both threat and means of rescue. A young girl
throws herself overboard from a ship. It seems certain she will
drown, but the positive and hopeful approach is revealed
through the decisive action of her lover. He dives into the
water and swims strongly and saves her. So here is another
swimmer who shows that man can live by facing the pressures
of nature with creative understanding. The narrator comments:
'Water is a friendly element for the man who is familiar with
it and knows how to handle it. It bore him up, and the skilled
swimmer was its master.'

We know about our origins in the sea, about the fertility
of rivers, about changes in the face of water as it moves from
calm to storm, changes which seem to correspond to fluctua-
tions in the human spirit as man veers between those extremes
of classical discipline and romantic dissolution. Our consciousness is fluid. When the poet uses water as an image of man's
experience he is simply doing his usual job of transforming
known fact into symbolic truth. The known fact is that everything flows. Our consciousness is fluid because everything we
experience is fluid.

This fluidity is perilous. We can drown in it. There seems to
be no foothold here. For survival we need certainty, so we
look for it and we create it where it does not exist. We edit

the shifting particles of our experience into comforting form. We make the tablets of law and walk on them, choosing the paths of righteousness for our daily defence, not because we happen to have read the Old Testament. On these paths we find security, solid ground of habit. This is one way of handling the water of experience—by pretending it does not exist as water but only as a static face. We can hardly say this is the way to become familiar with it. We treat it as a hostile element, we turn our backs on the sea like the traveller who takes to the mountain tracks for his protection. Yet it is the walk on the water which is offered to us as the way of life.

In Goethe's book Ottilie cannot take to the water. When she does, it is in panic, not with faith, and the result is disaster. Her usual path went round the water, the path (as she implies) ordained for her by society. Leaving this safe path and trusting herself to the mystery is equivalent to breaking the law, her laws. But of course she does not really place her trust in the unknown, she tries to take advantage of it. She is not familiar with it, she does not know how to handle it, so she is over-whelmed. The lesson is clear: limited human consciousness should, for its own protection, keep to the prescribed and known paths, those paths which do not go over the water. How then can the walk on the water be offered as the way of life?

It is not said that life and our knowledge of it are the same. The map of human association shows us many well-tried and relatively safe paths. They keep clear of the water, where the familiar melts into mystery. But the mystery exists and challenges. Can truth be derived from a deliberately partial view of experience? The hostile element becomes friendly when we are familiar with it—not with a part of it but with the whole. It becomes friendly when we see the connections which give form to the apparently formless and link finite particles in flow. There is no infinite. This is the confidence trick which robs us of confidence. Fluid nature consists of finite, specific cells. Everything flows, but the flow is architecture.

In every waking moment we face a new flood of impressions. How do we maintain the human posture, how do we move forward with a human step on this torrent? We must move forward if we are to belong to the stream of natural energy. All human effort beyond the social and defensive is an effort to tread a pathway on this water, to find a coherent sequence in a world which seems incoherent. And this is the paradox: the pathway of truth is made of water. There is no other substance in our experience, if water stands for that whole hesitant realm which we now find incomprehensible. The writer (and not only the writer) wakes up every morning to attempt the walk on the water. We know a god can do it. He is the form which denies formlessness and expresses the coherence of all life.

To seek the footpath on the water is no doubt a great presumption, but a necessary one. Now we are observers of miracles. When we know that miracles are only commonplace connections of nature which are as yet beyond our understanding, we shall no longer be observers but participators, taking the natural and therefore fluid path of transformation. The miracle, like art, is the echo which comes to us in advance of the event.

The Tree of Movement

How to begin? Where to begin? Is there any more puzzling question for the writer? He could ask himself: why begin at all? But the fact that he is a writer is his answer to this question. He begins because he must, even without knowing where to begin, perhaps because he doesn't know where to begin.

'If you don't know where you're going, any road will take you there.' I came across that quotation at the head of a chapter in a book by Henry Miller. He doesn't say where he found it. I think it's a first cousin to the saying that all roads lead to Rome. If you don't know where you're going, *any* road will take you there. So you start. But that's no answer. Nobody tells you which road to choose, where to begin. Do we perhaps take that celebrated advice to begin at the beginning, go on to the end, then stop? Even this doesn't tell us where the beginning is—or the end either. Tristram Shandy manages to write his way into the middle of Book IV before he is even born. Or perhaps you would like to start at the other extreme and get the end over first? Machado de Assis begins his novel *Epitaph of a Small Winner* with a chapter called 'The Death of the Author'.

Birth and death have nothing to do with it. Wherever the writer begins, he is trying to find what Eliot calls 'the still point of the turning world'. 'At the still point, there the dance is, / But neither arrest nor movement.'

The dance has been called the mother of all language. Everything moves, but movement which seems arbitrary and disconnected is confusing. So we try to define it, to give it shape. Dance is definition, a pattern drawn from movement, human assertion of style. The steps connect, the gestures flow into each other. Everyone knows that words too can be pattern, following the feet of the dance.

The essential thing about style in any sphere (dance, words, clothes, or the way you walk down the street) is that it is a flow which has form, or a form which flows. Every object in nature has style. Here everything moves, everything has energy; natural form occurs where there is a transitory balance of energies. Fields of force exist even without iron filings. Turner made them visible in paint.

This form is delineation. It's not fixed (nothing in nature is fixed), it's fluid still and ready for transformation, which is inevitable movement to a new form, the next step in the dance. Style is the same as form in nature: it is movement given illusory stillness. The impression made on us by style is of effortless and even aggravating ease. This is because there is no visible effort. We are looking at a balance of tensions, an apparent island of firm ground in the restless energy which moves every particle of our being and everything that surrounds us. Yet this island too is made of energy and movement. It can be made of nothing else. All that exists is formed of energy. The material moves—that's why it's so hard to begin. But delineation can come only from movement. So we begin.

Rilke describes a dancer in one of his Sonnets to Orpheus. This is a poem about the connection between human style and natural form. It is the climax of the dance, the girl is spinning in one spot. Rilke speaks of her now as 'a tree made of movement'. He transforms her: a human pattern of movement becomes a tree, a natural form. The speed of movement makes her look like a still surface—an optical illusion we can all appreciate. This is delineation from movement, a tree made of movement. Of course, every tree *is* made of movement even if this is not perceptible to us—as the movement of the dancer cannot now be seen as movement.

This solid flesh does melt, the form flows, the flow presents itself as form. Before our eyes, Rilke's dancer flows from human form to the form of a tree to the form of a vase spinning on the potter's wheel. One shape runs into another, as it does all the time in nature. Pattern emerges from the moving material. The fluid is given form, the static is sensed to be fluid, at the still point of the turning world, neither arrest nor movement. Form . . . in stone, cloud, poem, in man. There the dance is, but neither arrest nor movement. What Eliot means is that it is neither simply arrest nor simply movement, but both, the form which flows, the flow which has form. Here is the still point of the turning world, the still point of the turning dancer, the tree of movement.

The writer begins because he wants to give form to what has up to now seemed formless. Style, which is form, must be started, found in the only thing which exists—which is movement. The writer begins as nature begins, he shapes form by diverting energy which is already there, as water swirls into a fresh pattern when you put a stick in the current. Pattern emerges from the only possible place, from the moving material.

Laurence Sterne puts his own stick into the water. In *Tristram Shandy* he tells us that '. . . of all the several ways of beginning a book which are now in practice, I am confident my own way of doing it is the best—I am sure it is the most religious—for I begin with writing the first sentence—and trusting to Almighty God for the second'.

At first glance, this doesn't look like the most religious way of doing it, since it puts Laurence Sterne first and Almighty God second. This order might not have appealed to St. John. He had his own ideas about the first word. All art is a kind of presumption: it implies criticism of accepted order. But it is not criticism of creation. It springs from dissatisfaction with man's view of creation.

In the beginning was the word. The writer is looking for that word. He is starting creation all over again—but this is what is happening in nature all the time. Goethe's Faust is translating the New Testament, and it's not by chance that when we see him he is wrestling with this opening verse from St. John. He too is looking for the beginning, a way to make understanding contact with nature. How does creation work? This is his question. Now he has returned to his study after experiencing the joys of spring and the pleasures of the open air, nature, and natural people.

'It is written', says Faust: 'In the beginning was the word.' This translation doesn't satisfy him. He tries again. 'It is written: In the beginning was reason.' This won't do either. He thinks of a third interpretation of *logos*: 'In the beginning was power.' He is still not satisfied. In his despair he cries: 'May the Spirit help me!' And the Spirit does help him. He sees clearly what he has to write: 'In the beginning was action.'

This action which is in the beginning is like all life—it is movement. Action is not only in the beginning, it is always and everywhere. Everything moves, everything flows, each form melts into future possibilities. So how can we speak of a beginning, or an ending? We must recognize that to start and to finish are convenient human conceptions, products of our thirst for definition. Life goes on, and the only truth is movement. This is the sense of the Lord's promise, in Goethe's play, that salvation will be granted to the man who constantly strives. Faust, in his foolish meanderings, always comes back to this truth, discovered from St. John, that creation is action and man too must move with the flow. There is no convenient cage for truth. Every beginning emerges from the past, each apparent ending dissolves into the future. The line is continuous.

Günter Grass begins his *Cat and Mouse* in the middle of a sentence. This is his way of saying there is no beginning in our definite sense. 'How shall I begin?' asks Oskar Matzerath, the dwarf narrator of Grass's novel *The Tin Drum*. The storyteller in *Cat and Mouse* comes to the point where he says: 'Who will write me a good conclusion?' There are no volunteers. There is no conclusion, no full stop in experience. This is the form which flows.

How then does the writer begin, if there is no beginning? How does he make creative contact with the flow? Delineation can come only from movement, and you join the movement of life simply by moving. In the beginning is action. Faust decides on this translation of *logos* after discarding other possibilities—the word, reason, power. But does he discard them? Action does not eliminate the other possibilities, it is superimposed on them like a mask. They are still there. Action contains them. We are speaking of creation, where action creates the word and reason and power.

It is not too difficult to accept the word and power as products of action, but are we to believe that first we act and then we find the reason? As an implication of *logos*, reason is logical connection between aspects of our experience. Those aspects which are not connected in our consciousness seem irrational—absurd or magical (the choice is ours). As soon as we see connections, then the matter is reasonable. What is art but the making of connections which have not been visible up to now? The writer makes form, and form is the visible presentation of a shape in movement, a tree of movement. If the beginning is action, not reason, it is because action is the dance which joins one step to another to find a pattern in movement.

Art reaches out for patterns which lie outside immediate understanding. The writer surprises himself as much as anybody else when he gives form to what has seemed formless, without logical connection. He works from the frontier which, according to Kafka, stands between daily life and the terror which seems more real. 'My life is a hesitation before birth,' says Kafka; and elsewhere in the diaries, 'Not yet born, and already compelled to walk the streets and talk to people.' Here he acknowledges that for him life is partial perception, incomparably dark but the womb of truth, since it is the writer's only point of departure.

c

The writer can't see the pattern. It cannot be calculated in advance. All that is given is this place and this time. The pattern develops as he works his way across that frontier into the moving material. This development is revelation. This new form, the tree made out of movement, is linked to his point of departure, since the beginning can be nowhere else. If reason is visible connection, he has now uncovered reason, and he has found it through action. The activity of the writer is itself the connection.

In the work of art, reason is inexplicable, faint, sensible only to the eye of feeling. The impression made by the new form is of truth which cannot be understood yet is understood. We recognize what we have not seen before, and we recognize it because it is related to what we know. Samuel Butler tells us in his notebooks that there is no mystery about art. 'Do the things that you can see,' he says; 'they will show you those that you cannot see. By doing what you can you will gradually get to know what it is that you want to do and cannot do, and so to be able to do it.' Delineation comes from movement, the invisible is suddenly seen. It was there all the time.

There is nothing more splendid in Rilke than his praise for the fertility of human senses, whose only material is the productive earth of our experience. The world available to our senses is the point of departure, so the beginning must be here, and Rilke proclaims it. Again and again this poet emphasizes that he works from the physical, from feel of rope, taste of an orange, from the shapes of nature tangible to ear and eye, the sensual urgency of life moving in all its forms. This is the marvellously multiple world of 'fresh-firecoal chestnut-falls' celebrated by Gerard Manley Hopkins. '*Here* is the time of what can be said,' says Rilke in the ninth Duino Elegy. By '*here*' he means this place, this earth, this time. He expresses it as a place which is a time: '*Here* is the time of what can be said, *here* its home. Speak and proclaim.' This is his command to himself, to the writer. He must speak and proclaim.

Virginia Woolf saw life as impressions falling on a luminous halo of consciousness. No fixed beginning, no fixed end, only movement. In fiction the stream of consciousness leads only too often into dreadful rivers of tedium, but the fundamental assumption is right: the assumption that nothing is unimportant, nothing accidental. Everything matters. Every detail is part of the whole movement of experience. There are connections we cannot yet see. Wherever the writer begins, he is, through that action and because it is action, making contact with the natural movement of all life. How will it turn out? What pattern will emerge? He doesn't know and he can't know until he *makes* the pattern by putting his stick into the current. But this is choice. The writer asserts himself, as the organic cell asserts itself.

The writer is not a philosopher, he is a man of action. Even Napoleon tells us he had no definite plans, only projects. For the writer, the project is the writing of the first sentence. That first action is the beginning which emerges from the past, so it is shaped by circumstance, the circumstance which is the situation of this writer in his time and place.

Napoleon goes on to say he didn't try to control circumstances, he obeyed them, and they forced him to change his mind all the time. This is organic behaviour. Reason emerges from events. This is how the man of action becomes a man of destiny: he allows the present to shape the future. The new shape is the accident which is allowed for, prayed for even, but which can never be calculated. If a writer is really a man of destiny he gets the accidents he deserves. And he deserves them because he acts without knowing where he is going. He begins by writing the first sentence and trusting to the almighty flow of life for the second.

The hero of Scott Fitzgerald's novel *The Last Tycoon* is flying across a range of mountains. He sits by the pilot and looks down at the hills. 'Suppose you were a railroad man,' he says. 'You have to send a train through there somewhere. Well, you get your surveyors' reports, and you find there's three or four or half a dozen gaps, and not one is better than the other.

You've got to decide—on what basis? You can't test the best way—except by doing it. So you just do it.' The pilot doesn't understand. He thinks he has missed something, so the man says: 'You choose some one way for no reason at all—because that mountain's pink, or the blueprint is a better blue. You see?'

Perhaps we do see. In another part of the novel Fitzgerald's hero complains that certain people are not equipped for authority. He means they are paralysed when there is no obvious reason for choice. He goes on to say: 'There is no substitute for will. Sometimes you have to fake will when you don't feel it at all. You have to say, "It's got to be like this—no other way"—even if you're not sure. A dozen times a week that happens to me. Situations where there is no real reason for anything. You pretend there is.'

What matters is the first action, taken when there seems no real reason for it. This is Laurence Sterne's invitation to Almighty God, Faust's understanding of eternal beginnings. Wherever man touches the tangle of apparently unformed life he touches the flow which connects and carries. 'Of all the several ways of beginning a book . . .' Laurence Sterne's way is the most religious after all. It is an act of faith. It rejects the idea of accident, it expresses completely that mixture of humility and boldness which is the artist's nature. It springs from the certain belief that form can emerge only from flux, that there is pattern in the moving material, pattern which will respond to the gesture of the writer as he seeks the still point of the turning world, the tree of movement.

It is curious that the tree is one of the oldest objects of human worship. It shares this sacred position only with the snake—the stick that moves.

The Glass Bead Game

For the first time in my life I have come to a confession of faith. I believe in the impossible. Not only because the possible is daily becoming more terrible to conceive, or concede, but because I believe this is the only creative attitude. It is strange how one's gestures and impressions . . . I nearly said ideas, but they are not ideas. I know nothing about philosophy. I mean the physical fact of life, which is response to experience, gestures induced from sensations which seem so casual until suddenly they coalesce and direction is seen, if only for a moment. . . . It is strange and exciting to endure this kind of meaningful accident. Then one realizes that it is only through accident, which is revelation of some connection one has not seen before, that one lives. To believe in the impossible is to invite the co-operation of this kind of accident, the event which comes from outside the immediate definition of knowledge. I believe in the impossible because I do not see any other way to negotiate with the future.

I look back on a misspent youth. I was afraid of making mistakes. The immediate definition of knowledge was all-important to me, and I would not willingly go outside this safe circle. I realize now that my fear of making mistakes was the only real mistake. There are many ways of being right, and being wrong is one of them. It is a misfortune to be born with a strong sense of the ridiculous. Later it becomes a source of amusement, even of consolation, but in early life one is ignorant, one does not know that the ridiculous is a social attribute, a weapon of taboo. Then there is only one potentially ridiculous figure in the whole world—oneself. It is necessary to know the right action, which is the action confirmed as acceptable by one's schooling.

Formal education seems designed to persuade us that certainty is the only virtue. We are cursed with commandments which give the impression that because we are uncertain (and we know we are) we must be inadequate. So, in the circumstances, we feel we *are* inadequate. This is the source of guilt. I should like to see an education which teaches that the normal condition of man is uncertainty. This kind of education would not imply that we are fools if we are dissatisfied with the answers drawn from our circumscribed knowledge, nor would it assign the indefinable to some careful category of revelation sealed off eternally to human logic. Belief in the impossible is acceptable if you call it religion; it becomes eccentricity when adopted as a principle for daily conduct. This education would deal with the fantastic; that is, with life. It would ask questions for which there are no final answers, since every living form is a speculation. These are the only questions worth asking, and our constant uncertainty asks them, without words. Uncertainty is growth, and growth is constant.

But only the knowledgeable man can ask these questions. Projection into the future is organic and cannot grow out of nothing. It develops from the precise present, as all the fantasies of the human imagination spring from observation of available fact. We are like players in a game who start from a basis of knowledge and skill. This basis matters, it is the beginning of discovery, but only the beginning. We have drawn this knowledge and skill from past experience, but we do not live in the past, we live in the present. We have not touched this point in development before. Everything has changed, because growth is change. We find we must bring into play that flexible pursuit of possibilities which we call imagination, the pursuit which begins from what we know but takes us beyond it. This is where the possible shades into the impossible which can be realized through action we have not been taught. This is what I mean by our negotiation with the future.

For this game we may be superbly well equipped and well trained; every move from the past may be known to us; but no human intellect can anticipate the nature, let alone the sequence, of all the permutations of experience which can now develop. There are too many possibilities, factors, counters, accidents. They change shape and position, they influence each other, we influence them. This is the unpredictable play of forces in which we exist and to which we contribute. Nothing is ever still, nothing is ever quite what it was. The game is movement. Everything happens quicker than thought, because the new situation (and every situation is new) has not yet been captured by thought. It is beyond the intellect. It requires action we have not consciously learned, so we don't think, we just do it. Training is transmuted into instinct. The creative player responds flexibly and accurately to changing circumstances as they are revealed, and this balance of fantasy and precision is crucial. From it comes the connection we have not seen before, the creative accident.

Hermann Hesse wrote a novel about this particular kind of game which blends precision and fantasy. In *The Glass Bead Game* the glass beads themselves stand for both the mathematical units of the abacus and the hieroglyphics of musical notation. This suggests that the musical flow of instinctive response is the material of mathematical design. Shape emerges from action. In the novel these beads are moved into fresh patterns to represent the game of life—or life as it is discovered in the place where this mysterious game is played. For it is mysterious; we are never quite sure of the rules of the game or of the method of play. This is remarkable, because the author appears to describe them in detail. He convinces us there are rules, that there is a strict and traditional method of play. He seems to be explicit, but he is not. This is a triumph of the novelist's art, for here he is both precise and fantastical, presenting an image of the moment which is accurately detailed but which cannot be defined because it is open. He reflects the uncertainty of life itself. Are we ever quite sure of the rules of *this* game?

Hesse's story is set in the future. It is told by a narrator who looks back from an even more distant future. His subject is the life history of a man called Joseph Knecht who becomes master, or director, of the glass bead game. The game itself is an important activity, a kind of religious institution, in the imagined province of Castalia, which is really an aesthetic realm, remote from the real world but financed by it. It is run on benevolently authoritarian lines. It has its own organization and hierarchy, something like a monastic order. Here the individual counts only as part of the total pattern and effort. As, of course, the individual move in the game counts only as part of the revealed design. The game itself turns out to be a symbolic vision of interrelationships. We are told that the idea of the game is 'eternally present'; it is 'a path from potentiality to reality', 'a sublime art and science', nothing less than 'a mode of playing with the total contents and values of our culture'.

In other words, it is based on total known experience, immediately available. This is the stock of glass beads moved in the game to produce 'a kind of world language for thoughtful people'. The suggestion of language implies definition. Is this language any different from the one we know? If culture is a conclusion about experience, a conclusion put into practice in civilized behaviour, the glass bead game is meant as a complete and coherent view of this culture; but a view which changes as the game progresses and yet is harmonious in every variation. Individual counters are ideally parts of a unity which is never final. The game is a search for harmony in a world experienced only as individual detail. The glass bead is the finite cell, the sacred fact, the sole basis of the changing collaboration of forces which we call life, the form which flows. This game is movement, as life is movement and the discovery of form in and through movement.

We are told that everything in the glass bead game leads to the centre, away from the single example to 'the mystery and inmost heart of the world, to primal knowledge'. The separate detail is therefore only the beginning. Known experience is the potential which must be developed before the player can move into the unknown, the new form. Joseph Knecht, the master of the game, sums it up like this: 'Each transition from major to minor in a sonata, each transformation of myth or religious cult, each classical or artistic formulation was . . . if seen with a truly meditative mind, nothing but a direct path to the centre of the cosmic mystery where holiness is constantly being created in the alternation of inhaling and exhaling, of heaven and earth, and of Yin and Yang.' In this region opposites are not opposites but necessary components of harmony. So the game is called not merely a world language but also 'a sacred and divine language'. The divine is a particular interpretation of the familiar.

'If seen with a truly meditative mind . . .' Meditation is an essential part of the game. The name *Knecht* means servant, serf, one who submits. The master of the game submits to experience as it develops. This is the secret of his skill. The greatest obstacle to understanding is the mind which judges solely on the evidence of past knowledge. Such a mind is lost in a new situation, which then becomes impossible. Joseph Knecht is open to the unknown, he does not impose himself on knowledge, he lets knowledge come to him, he responds flexibly to changing circumstances as they are revealed. His actions may seem accidental at the time, but this means only that we do not immediately see connections with what we know. Truth is a proper respect for the accidental.

As a servant of experience Knecht responds without commitment. It is because he sets such value on spontaneous response that he comes to rebel against the game as institution. Organizers are not fond of change, once they have organized. It is not only in Castalia that the glass bead game is a public institution. Each country now has its Game Commission; above these boards is a World Authority, the only body allowed to modify the vocabulary and rules of the game. Such modifications, we are told, hardly ever happen. What kind of language is this, which cannot grow? An established system eliminates the individual, but the only worthwhile elimination of individuality occurs in creation, where the finite cell is caught in constant transformation and you lose your life in order to find it. Stop movement, and it is no longer a game; it is a frozen memorial. The form does not flow.

So we come to the perennial conflict between authority and freedom. Knecht is expected to suppress every individual impulse and submit to the discipline of his order, to the rule drawn from past experience. But instinct now asserts itself, his living instinct for change and growth, the instinct which says there is meaning in the attractive unknown. The glass bead game itself, the province, the hierarchy of officials and players—these have become traditional and sanctified. But the holiness is more apparent than real. This sanctity is a defensive gesture, the divine right of kings which has its source in human presumption. Knecht feels he has reached 'the point where great men must leave the path of tradition and obedient subordination and, trusting to supreme and indefinable powers, strike out on new courses where there is no path and where experience is no guide'.

That last phrase seems suspect. Experience is a guide. Not a complete guide, but the only one we have. It shapes our contribution to the unknown future form. This guide works blindfold, merged into the dark unconscious. Knecht takes with him what he has learned. Where could he leave it? He is a gambler who abandons the paths of rational prediction, but the starting point of the inexplicable is the known. The only root of the fantastic is the familiar. The impossible projection develops from original form, and this development is the speculative game which joins chance to certainty and accident to reason to build a new shape which is without chance, without accident. This shape is the impossible discovered as inevitable.

Napoleon knew that precision without fantasy is not enough. He said that in military science it is necessary first to calculate all the possibilities accurately and then to make an almost mathematically exact allowance for accident. The implication is that in some as yet invisible form of higher mathematics the accidental can be traced as discernible force and logically linked to the known. It is on this point of accident, said Napoleon, that one must make no mistake: a decimal more or less may alter everything. And for Napoleon this was not only the formula for success in war but the basis of all creative imagination. 'Now this apportioning of knowledge and accident', he said, 'can take place only in the head of a genius, for without it there can be no creation.'

Joseph Knecht feels he is trapped in a system which excludes accident. He is convinced of the Napoleonic truth that without a combination of knowledge and so-called accident there can be no creation. The glass bead game in its present state is sterile, an aesthetic ideal, an academic juggling of concepts. His province of Castalia depends on the outside world, the contemporary world of history, but it remains deliberately remote from this world because history is accident. This province is only part of the whole, and a detached part. How can there be partial truth? He feels he must escape if he is to find truth, he must turn to that other world, to the experience which is history. And the study of history, says one of the other characters, 'means submitting to chaos and yet holding on to faith in order and meaning'.

This novel was published in 1943, so Hesse's work on the book coincided with a time when, particularly for a German, history was both the greatest reality and the greatest irrelevance. Who could find order and meaning in this horror? But the novel is not an evocation or even a veiled symbol of that period. Knecht is simply an exemplary character who comes to realize he must face history, in the sense of all experience, the daily world of loose ends. He leaves behind those ritual moves which have become 'an empty exercise and formula'. He has to respond as an individual. He speculates because he is alive. He has to negotiate with the future in the only place where it is found—in the present, the chaotic present. There is no certainty here, nothing but the questioning face of experience. The only certainty is that he will gamble, for the game is movement. He believes he can realize the impossible.

The Druid and the Wren

AN Irish friend tells me she remembers going round with the boys in County Dublin on St. Stephen's Day. They would sing a song which began like this:

> The wren, the wren, the King of all Birds,
> St. Stephen's Day was caught in the furze.

The Christmas custom of hunting the wren was common at one time all over Europe. This Irishwoman also tells me the girls made sure the boys didn't actually catch a wren, but they were supposed to. They were supposed to catch it and kill it, hang it from a pole, and carry it from house to house. Ritual is older than human memory. It is hardly likely that any of these children could tell us why they were supposed to do this. Or why they called the wren, the smallest thing, the 'king' of all birds.

We tend to look on primitive man as an embryo, the beginning of a natural progress to our more refined state. We know more than he did. This is true, but it does not follow that we understand any better. Knowledge makes it more difficult to understand. We have problems of organization, problems which grow as knowledge increases. In the survivals of primitive man, in his stories (which are dances) and in his dances (which are stories), we see a state of human awareness instinctively closer to natural truth. Harmony in the natural world is connection between all forms of creation, between sticks and stones and man and beast. Animal masks and cave drawings have been interpreted as the hunter's means of identifying with the creature to be found and killed. But wasn't there perhaps a more personal magic here—an attempt to identify, really to identify, to sustain that almost forgotten link between man and animal in nature? In the Jataka stories the Buddha is regularly reborn as bird or beast as well as man; there seems no intrinsic superiority here in the human form. The form is simply a particular organization of common factors. Christ is born among animals; the human shape of divinity begins here, the link with animals presented as a natural feature, without condescension.

Science extends our awareness of the environment. It is not so long since we thought bats and dolphins were silent. Now high-frequency devices sharpen our ears. Who knows what wonders are still hidden in vibrations inaccessible even to our new perceptions? The present gap between man and animals is a product of specialization, of the urge of each cell to be different and individual. Folk-tales take us back to a vision of natural integration between Orpheus-man and animals and trees. But at the same time man's regretful knowledge of separation is reflected in the disturbance we call plot, those ripples of interest, doubt, and defiance which multiply as character conflicts with circumstance. Things do not always go well for man in these stories.

In the tales collected by the brothers Grimm, animals are a special source of truth. The faithful horse Falada, in 'The Goose Girl', continues to speak truth (to those who will hear) even when his head is cut off and nailed over the gate. Birds seem to have special wisdom, not only in these tales but also in religious ritual through the ages, from the sacred hawks of the Egyptians to the eagle lecterns of the modern church, where the bird seems the very fount of Scripture. Perhaps it is their flight which connects them particularly with the gods, as intermediaries between heaven and earth. In the Middle Ages birds were supposed to be able to divine royal blood, in this way to see truth hidden from mere man. In Caernarvon-shire there is a tradition that no bird will fly over a certain lake because a native Welsh prince was drowned there by his enemies.

Druids were wise men, leaders in religion, favoured with insight. It is said that in Ireland even the king might not speak before the Druids had pronounced on the matter. They practised divination from the cries of birds, and the one bird which seems to have been their special assistant was the wren. In Welsh *dryw* can mean both wren and Druid. Henry Rowlands, vicar of Tre'r Dryw in Anglesey, suggested an etymological connection in his *Mona Antiqua Restaurata* (Dublin, 1723). Perhaps his enthusiasm outran his etymology, but there is evidence of close association between this bird and this particular kind of man, and so between wren and magical knowledge.

Respect for the wren as bird of augury may account for his title 'king of the birds', common in many countries. An old story tells about the competition for the crown. The bird which can fly the highest will be king. The wren hides in the eagle's feathers on the way up and takes off from the summit of the other's ascent. Perhaps the title is an award for cunning (the word often used for 'wisdom' when it appears in an opponent). The smallest bird is conqueror, king, the key used by Druid-man in pursuit of truth. Confidence in the wisdom of the smallest thing may represent faith in the divine detail, the finite cell as the only basis of infinity, the trivial fact which threads through all transformations.

The story of the sacrifice and resurrection of the god-king runs through all human development. In Pembrokeshire the Druid was judge in legal disputes. If his verdict was questioned, he called on the wren to speak truth; from the judgement of the wren there was no appeal. This was truth, unshakeable. We are told that, as a result, a feeling of revulsion against the wren grew among the people of Pembrokeshire (which suggests they must have been an uncommonly guilty lot), and so began the immemorial custom of hunting the wren at Christmas.

Folk-lore gives many other reasons, so many reasons that we

can assume man does not know the reason; that life is the reason. The assault on truth seems to be a prime human obligation, the last resort of guilty men. So the god is sacrificed, torn to pieces like Orpheus, but never killed: he is there to be sacrificed again every year, as winter is a sacrifice of summer. The dead bird carried round on a pole by the boys of County Dublin or placed in a little house in the Pembrokeshire legend may not be actually torn to pieces, but in token he is, for the parade from dwelling to dwelling is a sign that each partakes of some fragment of the god. Truth is fragmented now, as we are fragments of the whole, and the killing of the god is a reconstruction of the original crime, the crime of separation from the harmonious truth of nature.

Folk-tales are set against this background of harmony. These birds and animals are intimate with truth because they represent a world without gaps in knowledge. If man were still naturally at home in that total world he would share this effortless understanding. The old tales tell of a transitional stage where man is conscious of separation but is not yet inexplicably remote from nature. He can still hear the language of animals, he accepts connections which seem impossible to us. Those who converse with animals and treat them as natural companions are rewarded, but those who revile them and are contemptuous of the confidences of nature in general are punished for human presumption.

In these stories animals help or hinder, but they infallibly help everyone who accepts them as truthful aspects of nature, however fearsome they may appear to human eyes. The frog-prince is an embodiment of opposites. His transformation into desirable lover is an assertion that 'opposite' is an illusion caused by imperfect human judgement. At first he is the repulsive aspect of life which sickens the princess; it is only when she accepts this aspect without reserve, without prejudice, that he 'changes' (it is her vision which has changed) and becomes his glorious 'opposite'. The opposite was there all the time.

Pins, millstones, eggs, and ducks can ride in a coach, just like Kovalev's nose in Gogol's story. Insects can speak, like the insect form of Gregor Samsa in Kafka's 'The Metamorphosis'. The most modern of our authors look back to the most ancient, joined in a common vision of integration, non-human as well as human. Nothing is irreconcilable, except to the judgement which relates everything exclusively to human needs and fears.

The prevalence of princesses in these stories indicates a class structure impossible in a totally integrated world, but the stories do not originate in a totally integrated world. They are human achievements and so, like every artistic creation of a new shape, products of dissatisfaction with the world as it is. These social differences are another separation. Class means classification, a further division into parts. Without separate elements there cannot be story, for suspense is opposition between strands. Harmony has no story.

These tales reflect both the world as it appears to man and the world as it might be. The apparent world provides the plot, the world as it might be supplies the resolution. Any true work of art is a paradoxical form which combines vision of harmony (in which there can be no separation) and recognizably in- dividual characteristics. But here the parts are coherent and speak of the whole, as the particular object in nature can be itself and more than itself. The artist delineates only through the individualism he is trying to transcend. We come to know his personal gesture.

In folk-tale the quest for form is expressed in magical resolu- tion of opposites, but opposites have to be stated before they can be resolved. Like all other aspects of man's insistent individuality, class structure is featured in the story only to be eliminated in that ideal existence which is here sensed and presented as final image. And the barrier of age disappears with the barrier of class. The rough old soldier who marries the youngest dancing princess has found his way into the stream of transformation which is the natural world. Here all things are joined and partake of each other. There are no opposites now,

D

only connected objects whose connection we do not normally see. Man is frog, lion is prince, the servant master. Time and place have no meaning where all is one. The only impossibility in this harmonious world is that any concept shall remain eternally its identifiable self. One shape slips too easily into another.

The trivial fact threads through all transformation. Bird or beast or dwarf speaks truth and tells the hero precisely what he must do to free his enchanted princess. These instructions are exact. The guilty cannot plead ignorance. Either you ignore truth, sacrifice the god, dismember the wren, or you listen to the voice of the smallest thing, the irreplaceable link in creation. Always, of course, the hero makes a mess of it at his first attempt. This is his human self; he knows better, he overlooks some trivial detail, an insignificant instruction. He is still in our world of relative values, separated from that realm where nothing is trivial, nothing insignificant. He succeeds only when he follows the instructions in every detail, acknowledging by his actions that the smallest thing is a vital constituent of the whole. He is given another chance (which is what we should like for ourselves, so it is written into the story) and as soon as he accepts the voice of truth, really accepts, letting things happen instead of trying to control circumstances, he wins through. He follows the chain all the way and finds it is the chain of trans-formation.

This chain joins different details together to form a simple line of development. The folk-tale sees connections where we see separation, it transforms diversity into unity. It is an arche-typal artistic form. The effort of art is also to redeem the sacrifice of the god by restoring dismembered parts into forgotten unity; it harmonizes apparently disparate detail. The flight of the fragments is magically reversed.

The intention of art has not changed since the primitive dance. Man looks for simple rhythms in a world which has become casually complex and inexplicable. It is the old choice between god of wrath and god of love, which is no choice at all except in the human mind. Opposites are a subjective classification of personal experience into concepts which live in the mind and nowhere else, a source of irritation because they correspond to the apparent world and do not correspond to the coherent world which might be. The magical country of folk-tale is not remote. We live in it, seeing present fragmentation and sensing impossible unity. It is form given to optimism drawn from grounds for pessimism. The irrational is by definition open and uncertain. Folk-tale is visible confidence that one interpretation of our experience can slip so easily into another that opposites dissolve. It is a matter of vision, of seeing what is not immediately there. Art is the vision which sees that simplicity is truer than diversity. The steps of this dance order the fragments of wrath into a formal pattern, a friendly god who speaks only through the smallest thing, the trivial step, the finite detail, the wren.

Foam on the Wave

ORIGINALITY is always surprising, not only because there is so little of it but because it speaks of a territory we have not seen before. Suddenly it is there, and that's all we can say; an eye has seen as if for the first time, a voice speaks in tones not heard until now. What makes the boldness of genius? We don't know. Perhaps an unusual chemical combination in the blood? If so, it was in the blood of Georg Büchner and may have been the source of the infection which killed him at the age of twenty-three. He was born near Darmstadt in 1813. He is remembered for three plays, a story, a subversive pamphlet, and an essay on the nervous system of a certain species of fish. Not much, but enormous.

Büchner was a scientist. He studied medicine, following his father, who was an important doctor in Darmstadt. But his interests went further, to zoology and philosophy, and he became proficient enough in comparative anatomy to obtain both a doctorate and a lectureship in the subject at the University of Zürich. In this short and active life the creative writings seem incidental, a kind of casual activity, but there is nothing casual about them; they connect directly with his scientific centre. 'I sit all day with my scalpel', he wrote to his brother in the last year of his life, 'and at night with my books.' He must have been writing with that scalpel. His literary works are dissections of the human condition carried out by a philosopher. The plays and the story are also essays on the nervous system of a certain species—man.

Scientist cannot be separated from poet in Büchner. The face of nature was of absorbing interest to him. As scientist he exposes facts, as creative writer he starts from them. There is nothing else. All the mystery and nightmare emerge from available fact, the unknown from the known; this is the progress of science, the leap of poetry. The visible is the only base for the pursuit of the invisible. So Büchner the writer starts from documents, the historical record, as Büchner the scientist starts from the specimen on the slab.

For his first play, *Danton's Death*, written quickly and secretly to raise funds for his escape from Darmstadt, he read every book and paper on the French Revolution he could find. This remained his method. His story 'Lenz' is based on the journal of a village pastor who described the madness of his guest for some months, the *Sturm und Drang* dramatist J. M. R. Lenz. Büchner's art is the statement of fact which becomes more than fact. His truth is rooted in recorded event which expands, as we see in his last work, the play *Woyzeck*. Here again he begins from reported detail, an actual person and an actual murder.

The person was Johann Christian Woyzeck, described in the record of the trial as a barber. He was more often a servant, and even more often out of work, drifting from one loathsome lodging to another in the poorest quarter of Leipzig. One evening in 1821 he made his mark on history by murdering his mistress. She was a widow who had other lovers, especially soldiers. He killed her with an old knife-blade; he had fitted it with a handle that afternoon before going to meet her. This seemed to rule out impulse, but Woyzeck claimed he had heard a voice telling him to stab and kill. He said he had heard other voices, seen strange things, fiery faces in the sky. In other words, it was not his fault; something outside him had made him do this. There was never any doubt that he was technically guilty. What concerned the lawyers and doctors was whether he was responsible for his actions.

Is man ever fully responsible for his actions? Büchner's Danton cries: 'What is it in us that whores, lies, murders, steals?' As if some irresistible force compels man to act in defiance of reason and morality. The story 'Lenz' is a realistic study of extreme irrational possession. Danton is not insane, yet he moves without resistance to his death, conscious of danger but helpless, as if pushed from behind by forces he cannot control and against which it is useless to struggle.

Büchner was close in time to the Romantic movement in literature, though no writer ever had less romantic frenzy. The Romantics were fascinated by the presence and power of the supernatural. They emphasized its constant impact by giving it form in nature, so that this threatening and compelling force seemed to be outside man, independent of him. In medicine there was a corresponding interest in deviations from normal perception and conduct—insanity, dreams, visions, compulsive acts, all the phenomena of irrational behaviour. The murderer Woyzeck became a notable object of scientific study, and from science he passed to Büchner and literature.

A doctor named Clarus examined Woyzeck in prison, not only checking his mental and physical state but questioning him at length about his past life. Clarus published his report in a medical journal and also, because of exceptional public interest, as a separate pamphlet. This is where Büchner found his play. He does not tell us this, but a comparison shows how he extracted incident and even, sometimes, phrases. Clarus advised the court that Woyzeck's delusions were not due to a defect of the mind, so the voices did not save him. He was executed in Leipzig in 1824.

Büchner's play telescopes the life of the real Woyzeck. The murder, committed when Woyzeck was forty-one, is of course the climax of the play, but now it is directly connected to an incident reported by Clarus which happened eleven years earlier. Woyzeck was then a soldier. He told Clarus he had had an illegitimate child by a girl who also had affairs with other men. He regretted having abandoned her. Büchner's plot must be one of the simplest in dramatic history. The common soldier Woyzeck (who is also a barber), thirty years old, is the father of Marie's illegitimate child; the Drum-Major seduces Marie; Woyzeck stabs her to death.

This is the framework of the known. On it Büchner builds images of the unknown. They make visible the state of mind of his principal character, for whom the world is incomprehensible, threatening, savage. What makes our actions? For Woyzeck it is a voice he hears everywhere, from the ground or in the wind. What he does seems to be imposed on him. Is man really a machine, triggered by some force outside himself? 'Marie,' says Woyzeck, 'there was something there again, lots of things. Isn't it written: And behold, there was a smoke coming from the land like the smoke of an oven? . . . It came behind me right to the town. Something we can't grasp, can't understand, something that drives us mad.'

Sometimes the voice speaks from the wall. 'Don't you hear it?' says Woyzeck to his friend Andres in the barracks. 'It says all the time "Stab! Stab!" and cuts me between the eyes like a knife.' He obeys the voice. Is he responsible for his actions? It is as though man is on the periphery of events, the helpless victim of some central invisible power. For Woyzeck the crust of the earth is thin, as thin as the crust of the human mind. He stamps on the ground: 'Hollow, do you hear? Everything hollow down there.' Büchner is fond of this image, the frail barrier ready to crack and release the monsters lying in wait. Woyzeck sees them. They are already in his world—destructive fire from heaven, toadstools growing in strange patterns, a head which rolls on the ground. Horror is human reaction to experience, and in Woyzeck horror takes physical shape.

Woyzeck is not mad. If he were mad, the play would be pointless, without general significance. There are people in the play who suggest he is on the brink of madness, and this is true. But it is true of everyone who tries to reconcile observed fact with the idea that the universe exists for human convenience. It is not truth that drives people mad, it is falsehood. Disappointment depends entirely upon expectation. Woyzeck is crushed, baffled, miserably poor, but not mad. Nor is he vicious. Büchner gives him quite a different character to that of the real-life murderer. A freak cannot be representative, so in the play Woyzeck is an affectionate father, an obedient soldier, a religious man. He has all the qualities of virtue, as we understand it, yet he becomes a murderer. After he has killed Marie he fears the consequences; he tries to hide the blood and get rid of the knife. He knows about morality, he knows he is doing wrong. But is he responsible for his actions?

Büchner grew up in a small German state where the division between rich and poor seemed an act of God kept in force by the secret police. He was politically active as a student. This was dangerous; friends were arrested and left to wither in prison. No executions, only torture, madness, suicide, or slow extinction. 'We have such a humane government: it can't stand the sight of blood,' wrote Büchner to his parents. He himself narrowly escaped arrest by leaving the country. It is not surprising that his view of the world was so dark. Everywhere he looked he saw injustice and suffering. Worst of all was the apathy of the oppressed. This seemed incredible yet had to be believed, because it was fact. They resisted revolutionary ideas and submitted to the will of their rulers as if to the will of God. If this was the will of God, it was the will of a god of wrath, not of love.

As a political revolutionary, Büchner was a failure. A fortunate failure for literature: the plays are power sprung from impotence. They begin from the conviction that there must be some historical force which keeps the poor in subjection. From this it is only a step to the fatalistic belief that man in all his actions is subject to uncontrollable powers. These powers are not friendly. Why should they be? Friendly or hostile is a subjective judgement, a measure of convenience.

Büchner wrote his subversive pamphlet when he was a student. In it he asked why the poor should feel bound by rules of morality made to preserve the special position of the rich. The poor live in a different world—and this is where Büchner places Woyzeck. The rules of behaviour are not the same. But this is not a play of social protest, except incidentally. Büchner's brilliant stroke is to use Woyzeck's social position as a means of withdrawing him naturally from under the cloak of conduct which morality imposes on impulse. Woyzeck is man bare of commitment, isolated among elemental forces. He is a different species from the captain and the doctor, these representatives of education and privilege. And he knows it. 'Poor people like us— Look, Captain, sir: money! money! If you haven't any money . . . We don't get a chance in this world or the next.' And when the Captain reproaches him with having no sense of decency, he replies: 'Yes, Captain, sir, decency. I don't have so much of that. We common people, we don't have decency, we follow nature's call. But if I was a gentleman and had a hat and a watch and an overcoat and could talk proper, I'd be decent all right. Must be a fine thing, decency. But I'm a poor blighter.'

Woyzeck seems to be talking about some foreign country he has vaguely heard about. He is dressed and trained for his role in society. When he goes with Marie to the fairground they see two performing animals, a monkey dressed as a soldier and a horse trained to count. These are images for Woyzeck himself, as everything in the play is expressive of his state of mind. The showman parades the monkey in front of the booth: 'Look at this creature as God made him—nothing to him, nothing at all. Now see the effect of art—walks upright, has coat and trousers, has a sword. The monkey's a soldier. That's not much: lowest form of human life.' When the horse is brought forward, his connection with human existence and with Woyzeck in particular is made equally explicit. 'This is a person, a man, an animal man—and yet a beast,' says the showman. At this point the horse obeys the call of nature, and the opportunistic showman cries: 'What that means is: man, be natural! You are made of dust, sand, dirt. Do you want to be more than dust, sand, dirt? Look, what powers of reasoning: he can do arithmetic yet can't count on his fingers. Why? Just can't express himself, just can't explain. He's a transmogrified human being.'

And then Woyzeck, the man who can't explain, this camouflaged monkey, this horse which obeys the call of nature in the middle of his 'rational' performance, is given a third image which seems to place him in the category of human machine. He becomes a walking biological experiment. Or are we always walking biological experiments? Büchner's irony has a way of turning round and staring at us.

Woyzeck has been paid by the Doctor to exist on a diet of peas, so that the results may be scientifically examined. His reactions are checked periodically. He is a laboratory specimen, an experimental subject. Emotion too becomes merely a measurable and interesting phenomenon. When Woyzeck is angered, the Doctor observes him with scientific pleasure. This is the devastating moment when Woyzeck realizes Marie is being unfaithful to him. 'Give me your pulse, Woyzeck, your pulse!' says the Doctor. 'Short, violent, skipping, irregular . . . Facial muscles rigid, tense, with occasional twitching. Deportment agitated, tense.'

Even suffering can be filed in the card index as a set of physiological responses. There is an echo of Clarus's cold report here. But it is the Doctor who is the machine, not Woyzeck; it is the Captain who is the mechanical moralizer; it is the Drum-Major, with his overwhelming physique and passion, who is the unreflecting destructive impulse. Woyzeck is none of these. Woyzeck thinks; and, because he thinks, he suffers. Büchner gives him a characteristic which differentiates him from the others. It is the attribute which, for Büchner, makes Woyzeck human and representative—he feels pain.

His pain is Büchner's pain, the disillusion of a man who hoped for a better world. After reading about the French Revolution he wrote to his fiancée: 'I felt as if I had been crushed by the horrible fatalism of history. I find in human nature a frightful sameness, in human relationships a force which cannot be averted, given to all and to none. The individual just foam on the wave, greatness a mere accident, the sovereignty of genius a puppet-play, a ridiculous struggle

against an iron law. To recognize this law is our highest
achievement, to control it impossible.'

If greatness is mere accident, failure is accident too, crime
an accident. Büchner's iron law is 'nature's call' which Woyzeck
is powerless to resist, something imposed on him as the
strange, tormenting phenomena which fill his experience. The
process is seen as meaningless, because the faith which believes
in harmony is missing. Our traditional legends are myths of
connection; in these we have images of sensed forces invisible
to the conscious mind, but images joined by faith into creative
causality. They are illogical meaning made visible. In this play
the grandmother tells the children a story which is Büchner's
idea of myth. It must be the most desolate fairy story ever told.
Now there is no hope of meaning in the incomprehensible:

Once upon a time there was a little boy and he had no father and
no mother, everybody was dead, and there was nobody left in
the world. Everybody dead, and he went and searched day and
night. And because there was nobody left on the earth he thought
he'd go to heaven, and the moon looked at him so kindly. And
when he finally reached the moon, it was a piece of rotten wood.
And then he went to the sun, and when he came to the sun it was
a withered sunflower. And when he came to the stars they were
little gold midges stuck up there like the shrike sticks them on the
blackthorn. And when he wanted to come back to earth, the earth
was an upturned pot. And he was all alone. And then he sat down
and cried, and he sits there still, and is all alone.

This story could be called central to the play, were it not that
everything in the play is equally important. It is a dark conclusion drawn from disappointment and therefore from
expectation. The world is undoubtedly dead, if we expect from
it human feeling, love and friendship. The universe is indifferent to these, and we have known it ever since Copernicus
removed man from the centre. What Büchner forgets to mention
is that it is this same 'nature's call' which has made him write
the play. He is talking about the unknown and compelling.
It is the source of genius too, the accident of greatness which
requires the co-operation of the unconscious in work that can

never be willed, producing effects beyond the range of the rational mind and therefore beyond any humanly perceptible cause. Creation itself is the accident of greatness. In nature it is eternal causality; to man it seems a combination of conscious and unconscious, because there is a part he cannot account for. Irrational fear is the price we pay for irrational hope, since both acknowledge the existence of events outside human explanation.

Woyzeck was put together some time after Büchner's death from two chaotic drafts found in his papers. These are sketches, scrawls. Pages are loose, not numbered, there are few clues to show what the dramatist had in mind for the final draft. There are obviously events in the play which establish a rough order of scenes: you can't have the murder at the beginning. This still leaves some scenes which may be inserted almost anywhere. Perhaps this is appropriate for a play which is about inevitable accident. The producer himself has to respond to 'nature's call'; he too must listen to the voices from the earth—or the text.

There is another reason why the order of scenes is sometimes unimportant. In this play Büchner developed a technique which was new. His structure is like a spider's web; the passive hero sits in the middle, and from him radiate the segments which are scenes. Not scenes in the normal sense of progressive action but images of experience. Take them in any order and they are equally important, equally centripetal. The only difference is that it is not the spider who is lodged at the centre, commanding his world, but the fly, helpless. Whichever way he turns, the human victim sees a different aspect of the action which is his present situation. Man's experience is always and only the present situation.

These scenes are Woyzeck's experience, his feeling, his pain, projected into bold word-patterns, like woodcuts carved out of language. This play is not about ideas; it is a sequence of shapes which moves us beyond rational reserve and familiar idea. Büchner's achievement was to devise a technique which is indivisible from Woyzeck's perception of life.

The German Expressionists rediscovered this technique in our century. They gave the play its first stage performance—in Munich in 1913, exactly 100 years after Büchner's birth. It excited them because it said what they wanted to say. They never said it any better themselves. The technique has spread into other forms. Gottfried Benn described a novel of his as 'formed like an orange'. What is an orange but a spider's web filled out with flesh? Benn meant that his chapters were segments round a central core, the subjective individual. The shape, the technique, reveals the nature of the experience. And the technique is now recognized as relevant because the experience is relevant.

It is the experience of man in the modern world. Woyzeck moves in an atmosphere which is primitive and mysterious but also modern, because, when all explanations have been offered and all knowledge tabulated, we still face an open and mysterious world. Our interpretation depends on how we look at things. Büchner had his own way of looking at them. That letter to his fiancée about the accident of greatness continues like this: 'It doesn't occur to me to bow down before the performing horses of history.' Where did his boldness come from? He possessed the necessary artistic talent of having no respect for the dead, especially when they are still alive. He stepped back from the mask of everyday values and left it in the air, empty, unreal, a thin covering of posturing and farce. And what he found and presented, ruthlessly, was an image of man recognizable in our day. We know Woyzeck. He still faces an incomprehensible world, he is trivialized by machines but has blood and emotions; he seems to be swept along by forces he cannot control and is desperately alone, mere foam on the wave.

Hellfire and Incense

It was not a politician who said the devil has all the good tunes. No politician could ever be so generous to the opposite party. When it comes to elections the simple political approach gives us a clear choice, the alternative of god or devil. And who would choose the devil when he has god for a candidate? Nobody but that benighted lot on the other side who are always mistaking hellfire for incense.

So we vote for god, our god. We put the cross on the ballot paper, the definite cross, this formal arrangement, one line crossing another. It is strange that we say Yes with a symbol which means No—or is this particularly appropriate to politics? There is no end to human ingenuity. The cross is an opposition of forces, a hostile balance, two lines locked in each other like the legs of wrestlers. We think we have defined order by making the cross, but in fact we have imposed order, arbitrarily; and this is what we are doing all the time. The cross acknowledges opposition, one line for, one against. It says: 'so far, no further'. There is no equivalent in nature. It is a human device, recognizably human for its certainty. Nature is always going further, but we do not live in nature; our institutions are angled and fixed. Humanity is perhaps a general tendency towards geometry.

Everything in nature which appears cruciform is really a development of side-roots, branches, cells. These arms are integral to the centre and flow from it. That other cross has been called the Tree of Calvary but it is not a tree, it's a human construction. The living tree is different: it grows, moves while standing still, changes in visible sympathy with the seasons and celebrates with us the cycle of birth and death and resurrection. It is metamorphosis, the flowing god, fount and shelter, the world tree. So when the god is killed, the tree is killed. There is no separation. Divinity is indivisible—it is in nature and of nature. The dead god is hung on a tree which is not a tree.

The cross of sacrifice is a direct angular opposition of horizontal and vertical. No tree ever grew like this. The horizontal says No to the upright thrust, and the No is denial of divine essence, as the cross is human denial of the flow of nature. This is where the bold individual hangs; the vote of society decides his destiny. We prefer the neat arrangement. There is no field of force about this 'tree' but only a memory, a vague sense of lost perfection. The institutional cross is a poor substitute for natural flow. Its laterals are not integral to the centre but point apart, to destruction. It is, of course, an instrument of torture.

In church architecture both tree and cross are celebrated. The Gothic vault, the soaring shafts, the dome, the arch, acanthus leaves, birds and squirrels in stone or wood on pillar and pew . . . we are in the sacred wood. And, with this organic image but separate from it, we find the instrument on the ground, the cross—the transepts at a cold right-angle to the nave. Tree and cross are together now, but still individual and separate. The killing of the god is represented here in floor and furniture, but above in the cupola of branches, in the flowing stone, we sense the persistent belief that the natural order is the home of divinity.

Opposites are only in opposition because they are connected. The association of opposites stands for something fundamental in human experience. We are beset by dualities. Everything enters us in couples, like animals going into the ark. Good and evil, pain and pleasure, life and death: the polarities seem to contradict each other, but so do male and female in those animals going into the ark, yet this is the only fertile combination. And combination is necessary to fertility.

We see the world around us in two different ways. In one way we see it as a random collection of separate objects and events; in the other we see more than we can see, we sense a wider experience, an imperceptible realm of truth. Art and religion are human reactions to experience; both affirm that truth lies beyond immediate perception. Through science we find physically that our perceptions can be extended and that there is material to match our enlarged vision. As the imperceptible is made visible, we may well feel that what is now our sense of glory may some day become verifiable fact. But until then it is, paradoxically, just this sense of glory which gives us our feeling of imperfection and doubt. Dissatisfaction is a gift of the gods. There must be something wrong with us: what we see is incomplete and what we sense is indefinable.

The incomplete is safer than the indefinable, but there's no satisfaction here either. 'Alas,' says Goethe's Faust, 'two souls dwell within my breast.' He finds this a cause for lamentation, and he is right. The two souls are the opposites which run through all human experience. Faust finds that part of him wants to cling to the earth, to the security of the known (if only partially known); the other part urges him to abandon safety and rival the gods. Known and unknown seem to be two opposing principles.

Who would choose the devil when he has god for a candidate? It seems that human beings would. The devil is familiar fragmentary experience, the god is that remote sense of glory. Our ancestral myths come back again and again, insistently, to the fate of men who want to be as gods, knowing good and evil. It's an eternal preoccupation. If it's punishment you want, then eat of the apple, strive like Prometheus, presume like Tantalus, fly like Icarus. We are told to behave ourselves, or we'll fall off the wall.

Mephistopheles, the fallen angel, originates in Paradise, but we know him as the image of imperfection. Isn't this also our idea of the human condition, squeezed between Eden and the Last Judgment? Imperfect, but promises to turn out well—which describes too our dual interpretation of the world, which is devilishly divided but the only home of the gods. This is why Faust follows Mephistopheles: the devil is that broken experience which Faustian man must endure as the road to truth. He is the only visible evidence. The rest is faith.

The hero of Hermann Hesse's novel *Steppenwolf* remembers Faust's claim to have two souls within his breast, because he feels like this himself. One side of him wants to run free in the forest of incoherent experience; the other is attracted by the secure restraint of life in family and society. He aspires to truth but is beset by division. He is the human conflict of light and dark, explicable and inexplicable, convenience and ambition, safetyman on one side, wolf on the other. When he thinks of the two souls, his conclusion is that Faust has simplified a complicated situation. Man does not have only two souls within his breast, he has a countless number. He is many facets, a sum of infinite and changing possibilities, inconsistencies which add up.

The human sense of glory is itself a vision of life as inconsistencies which add up. In the work of art too we see separate features as they appear in the perceptible world around us, but we are not now disturbed by incoherence. It is the apparently disconnected facts which produce harmony; there can be no other source. But connections are irrational here. We sense them to be true, without knowing why. It is the invisible connection which makes the work of art, so every work of art must be inexplicable. You can't explain it, you accept it.

The harmonious image in art is created from abnormal sensitivity to disharmony, the isolated detail. Without this sharpened awareness the effort would be neither necessary nor possible. The final form appeals to individuals for whom individualism is not enough. We know about individualism, it exists all around us, the world is split into parts. But we sense

E

connection and, what is more, we feel that connection is better than individual separation. The material of art is the divided world, the sense of art is a world without division. We are back at our duality. Both aspects, the apparent opposites, are present in the mind of the artist and in his creation. He is a man in his experienced world like everybody else. Art is a declaration that the separate elements around us are visible components of truth, that detail can and must be united in form, that inconsistencies do add up. Here the duality which plagues us is presented for what it is, not two opposing faces but two faces on a single mask, the indivisible world, irrationally connected.

But duality persists. We still see two faces, and it is only because we see two faces that the work of art can speak to us. There is in the work of art, as in the world outside, with all this sense of harmony, still a Mephistophelian variety of incident, plot, line, colour, sound. Taken separately, the individual characteristics of the work, as of our experience, may not add up; assembled by the artist, they speak of truth. It is this dual face on the single mask which makes the convincing structure of the work of art. This structure is a real physical, electric tension between particles, between individual characteristics. Here there *is* a field of force. It is alive, we are drawn into it, we share its energy. And it is made by this magical conjunction of 'opposites' which are now seen to support each other creatively. The work of art brings the two parts together to say Yes instead of No. The two parts are still visibly separate but uncannily one. This form is disciplined from the centre, organic, a flowing thrust.

Without a sense of harmony there would be no cohesion, without knowledge of imperfection there would be no incident, no plot. This is why the work of art, which should be an image of harmony, also manages to be individual and characteristic of its maker—it is *his* face, nobody else's. But while it acknowledges human imperfection it also stands for the truth that harmony must be made of individual parts, as every form in nature can consist only of finite and individual particles. The particular is the only representative of the whole; in nature and in art we see a representative individualism. Without individualism art would not speak to us. What we hear now is the language of imperfection, talking of higher things. The devil does have all the good tunes, if only because he has all the tunes audible to the human ear. From them we make up the songs of Paradise.

And what is Paradise? Is it something we once knew, and lost at the Fall of Man in the impossible past? Something we may perhaps know again in the remote future? Whatever it is, it is kept safely distant from us. The trouble with myths is that they can be so good, so representative, so habitual, that we allow them to do our living for us. We seem to prefer it this way— to make our inner dilemma an outer image and fix it for ever. Kafka tells us it is only our concept of time which makes us call the Last Judgment by that name; in fact, he says, it is a court in standing session. 'The moment is eternity,' says Goethe. They are both saying the same thing: that it's all happening now, here, nowhere else, no other time. Guilt and Paradise are our daily experience. They are simply that old duality, our knowledge of imperfection and our sense of glory. How are these compatible? The Kafka hero wakes up every morning to face life, as every man does, and he finds it's a court in standing session, an unending trial. He feels guilty without knowing he has done anything wrong. He cannot reconcile the two parts of his vision. This is the constant experience of man who senses harmony yet sees only inconsistencies.

All art is a kind of confident uncertainty. It's a declaration that form must come from formlessness, that Apollo is simply Dionysus organized. These gods, these apparently opposing principles, are tendencies we sense in ourselves. We have made them in our own dual image of the world around us. But the real triumph of human definition is that man has made chaos into a classical god. Or does this derive from unusual perception, some deep and ancient knowledge that the

Dionysian element of passion is divine too? It corresponds to our daily experience that form can come only from those scattered details which may be interpreted as disorder. Where there is vision, Apollo *is* Dionysus organized, the inconsistencies do add up. This is the union celebrated in art. And here, in art, the human gesture which finds form, we see a miraculous balance of separate individual characteristics, form made visibly from the components of chaos. It's from separation that harmony comes, it's from doubt that praise is constructed. Perhaps there isn't so much difference between hellfire and incense after all. And this fusion may be the real world, before our damnable philosophical tendencies get to work on it.

The Dilemma of Lord Chandos

THE son in Kafka's story 'The Metamorphosis' is an insect. Gregor Samsa wakes up one morning to find he has been transformed into a kind of beetle. Samsa/Kafka is infected with the dreadful certainty that he is unfit for life. He feels like an insect, so he is an insect. This writer makes pictures of feeling, and the feeling here is guilt. Can the pursuit of art be justified? The insect-form is an abdication of human shape; ultimately life itself is extinguished, the charwoman claps the lid of the dustbin on the shrivelled carcass. Samsa's family turns with relief to the normal round of daily existence, led by the father who has found new strength through his son's failure. In 'The Judgement' (all Kafka's fiction is self-judgement) an authoritarian father sentences his son to death by drowning. This is the verdict of life, and the son acknowledges the justice of it by becoming his own executioner. He drops off a bridge into the river: 'Dear parents, but I have always loved you.'

Kafka told a friend that Thomas Mann's 'Tonio Kröger' was his favourite story. It is Tonio who says literature is not a profession but a curse: 'A properly constituted, healthy, decent man never writes, acts, or composes.' The artists in Thomas Mann are near-criminals or diseased or deformed. Art becomes a peculiar and inescapable affliction which makes the sufferer unfit for normal society. Both Mann and Kafka long for the approval of their father-figure, authority. But the fate and feelings of their characters betray a sense of guilt which can only come from the fear that life may be truer than art, and defensive definition (represented by authority, our father in wherever he happens to be) a natural need of man. The father's anger is feared but accepted as right. The psychosomatic illness and psychosomatic insect are form given to the suspicion that the activity of art may be inadequate in itself. Thomas Mann's intense love of order is a German characteristic, a social and personal counterweight to that romantic passion and disorder which has also been characteristic of the Germans. If art too is part of the nihilism of our times, mankind may be better served by political and social discipline.

The special quality of the writer's despair appears in Hermann Broch's long novel, or poem in prose, *The Death of Virgil*. This is a work of art about the futility of art, an interior monologue which presents Virgil's thoughts and sensations in the eighteen hours before his death at Brindisi. Virgil wants to destroy his great poem. Through this figure Broch expresses his own sad conviction that art is inadequate as a means of perception. No human utterance, says Virgil, can 'disclose and announce the law . . . that knowledge beyond knowledge'. Absolute knowledge belongs only to supernatural powers and is closed to mankind; art is simply 'a fruitless effort and a blasphemous presumption'.

Broch's novel (1945) is a comparatively late statement. In October 1902 Hugo von Hofmannsthal published an essay which has come to be known as the 'Chandos Letter', from the name of its supposed author. This is the classic outline of the artist's dilemma. Hofmannsthal's essay is not written in his own name, but it describes his situation. The imagined writer of this letter is a certain Philip, Lord Chandos, an Elizabethan nobleman. In the past, Chandos (like Hofmannsthal) has produced precociously mature literary works, full of a sense of harmony. Now he has ceased to write, and this letter, addressed to Francis Bacon, is an attempt to explain his silence. He tells Bacon he has completely lost the ability to think or to speak of anything coherently. The reason is that he can no longer accept the relationship between himself and the world which has been habitual up to now. That earlier sense of harmony could be expressed in known language; the new relationship cannot. Where once he had seen the world as wholly integrated with his inmost self, he now sees detail and more detail:

Just as I had once seen part of the skin of my little finger through a magnifying glass, looking like an open field with furrows and cavities, so now I had a similar experience in relation to men and their activities. I was no longer able to comprehend them with the simplifying gaze of habit. Everything disintegrated for me into parts, the parts into further parts, and nothing could now be circumscribed by a concept. Individual words swam around me; they congealed into eyes which stared at me and into which I am compelled to stare back. These are whirlpools, and looking down into them makes my senses reel; they spin without stop, and through them one enters chaos.

So the collapse of old relationships is immediately tied to the expansion of knowledge, through the revelations of the magnifying glass, a parallel to his new and disturbing vision. The surface of language breaks up with the surface of the previously accepted world, for his language *is* that world, named and defined. It is the failure of language which is seen as vital, for the writer can still find irrational hints of glory in the parts which have split into further parts. When language is rigid it cannot cope with the elasticity of experience. He does not say it is men and their activities which confuse him; he is bewildered by isolated words, meaningless when disconnected, and in their very separation hostile to form, his own as well as the world's. Romantic grief is failure to connect when there is still awareness of possible connection. For Chandos remains tantalizingly on the brink of inspiration. He has the poet's sharpened sensitivity to the meaning inherent in commonplace objects and situations, but the magic name eludes him, so he despairs of language:

A watering can, a harrow abandoned in a field, a dog in the sun, a miserable cemetery, a cripple, a little farmhouse: any of these can be the vessel of my revelation. Each of these objects, and countless others like them, which we normally skim indifferently with our eyes, can assume for me at any moment (which I can by no manner of means summon up voluntarily) a sublime and moving character, for whose expression all words seem to me inadequate.

This kind of mystical experience is not uncommon. Things become their own symbols, charged with their meaning. Here is the beginning of inspiration, but only the beginning, in the moment (which cannot be willed) when perception is innocent. The effort of the poet is now to establish relationship through form, to change mystery into fact, which can only be presented in the hard surface of his material, language. But Chandos cannot go this far. He feels, but feeling is not art. The spiritual intensity cannot be transformed into words, at least not the words he has known up to now. There is a break between outer and inner, physical and spiritual, so he is sick, a victim excluded from the whole hale world. Chandos is representative, as his inmost self reflects the outer surface and, split into parts, takes its lack of meaning from it. But the gap between spiritual and physical is also present in the discontinuity between experience and language, as vague feelings of 'a sublime and moving character' flounder for lack of precise defining words.

It has not always been so. Once, the world of Lord Chandos was united, harmonious. This is a glimpse of Eden. No opposition between objects, and therefore no gulf between self and the world:

At that time, in a kind of permanent state of intoxication, the whole of existence seemed to me a great unity: the spiritual and the physical did not appear to me to be in opposition, and the same could be said for courtly and brute life, for art and non-art, solitude and society; in everything I felt the presence of nature, as much in the aberrations of madness as in the most extravagant refinements of Spanish ceremonial, in the boorish behaviour of young peasants no less than in the sweetest allegories; and in all nature I was aware of myself. . . .

This is the language of total acceptance, for Chandos deliberately includes extremes of behaviour which are coarse or ugly.

These too are man's experience, and the poet does not make exceptions for personal delicacy or social convenience. If he were to do so, he would be foolishly trying to achieve total connection while omitting integral parts. Any watchmaker could tell him what an impossible task that is.

This last sentence from Chandos goes on and on, long and involved, as if the complexity of life and its hidden connections can be expressed only in prose which is equally continuous and intricate. This is the road to the curiously complicated paragraphs of William Faulkner, whose sentences combine and expand like botanical capsules (defined in the dictionary as 'dry seed-cases opening when ripe by parting of valves'). Language takes on an organic similarity to experience even in the spare phraseology of Kafka when his clauses link interminably as he pursues truth from one junction of experience to the next in prose which quivers with new beginnings. In Broch's *The Death of Virgil* sentences roll unbroken for page after unpunctuated page until it seems impossible that Virgil can ever die. The convoluted sentence is an abstract of experience as it breaks loose in consciousness. It is complex because swollen with perpetual possibilities, one image developing into the next without a perceptible point of rest. Sanity is perhaps the ability to punctuate.

Chandos is no longer aware of himself in all nature. He is aware of himself as observer, separated from nature. But this is nothing new. Alienation is as old as Adam. The cherubim with the flaming sword defends the gate to Paradise. This dual image, of friend and foe in one, stands for the faith and despair conjoined in man when he looks at his surroundings. Man stands opposite, and he can interpret his experience either as the angel of kindly coherence or as the sword of visible fragmentation. Cherubim and sword are one image in the human interpretation of the world's face, the only gate of Eden. For Chandos the world wears both faces at once. He is tortured and charmed and, like every artist, he knows that his torture will end only when language spreads to join the fragments in harmony.

The writer is no different from any other man who is perplexed as fresh layers are stripped off the visible world and revelation becomes a synonym for confusion. Form disintegrates as knowledge breaks through boundaries. In another place Hofmannsthal defines the poet's task as purification and articulation of the material of life. But how can the poet purify and articulate what he cannot seize in the language of art? The despair of the present age, says Hofmannsthal again, is really loss of belief in form. We see the sword, not the angel. Discovery is movement. Either our definitions must keep pace with change or we are victims of circumstance, excluded like the Kafka characters who are always guilty because they are men.

Language is the agent of control and the means to mastery. It fixes the outside world in us. It is satisfactory as long as it shapes harmonious correspondence between outer and inner, the world and self. In such a state the author is linked to his surroundings in an ecstatic and productive relationship, as all nature is linked in fertile connection. This is surely what Kafka has in mind when he says the pen is not an instrument but an organ of the writer. Giving form becomes an existential necessity, since it also means (for the writer) taking form. 'Art is truth,' says Thomas Mann, 'the truth about the artist.'

Words are forced from the writer in a vital organic reaction. He must connect with his surroundings in order to realize himself, seeking his image in the world like Narcissus in the pool, but passing beyond that old lament for separation; he realizes himself by losing awareness of separate self, for there can be no separation where connection is total and harmony complete. Harmony is indivisible.

But what if the restless surface of the world shatters into particles which dart beyond the reach of known language? We like to think man is uncommonly disturbed in our times, and there is surely a bond between struggle in the streets and the multiplication of physical fact which is our daily experience. Where even our perception of fact seems fluid, authority in every sphere is suspect, for who can now define truth and claim to be its repository? But, although God was not officially declared dead until the nineteenth century, we are now experiencing no more than an acceleration of what has gone on ever since the first man climbed a hill and was forced to revise his ideas about his surroundings. If we are in a constant state of transition, it is because we correspond to the transitional world.

How do we connect with disruption? If the world has form, we are not able to see it. The optimist believes the collapse of external form is an illusion, the reflection of our failure to connect with the unknown, a condition which he hopes is temporary. The pessimist fears our inner turmoil may be a true image of a world which is a meaningless confusion of fragments. This is the sense of Hofmannsthal's idea that despair is loss of belief in form.

The phenomenon is seen daily to be free and elusive. But can the phenomenon be free if it is fixed in the word? Can language by its very nature be and remain as fluid as the shifting face of experience? Despair is the pessimistic certainty that a formless world cannot possibly be transcribed into the language of art, whose sole justification is the discovery of connections and the consequent delineation of form, the potent name plucked from the void. If language cannot do this, art is a pointless pursuit and a mere narcotic hallucination. Hofmannsthal expresses his doubts about the poet's vocation: 'What we call "Poet" is something arbitrarily bounded, like good and evil, warm and cold. . . . In nature there is nothing stable, limited, only states of transition.' When human utterance seems false, because inadequate, the only alternative is silent resignation. The meaningless individual becomes mute with despair.

Chandos falls silent when he loses the ability to think or to speak coherently. He is still sensitive to impressions but is not able to transpose feeling into form. Yet this inability to think coherently is no reason for silence, it is the reason for the utterance which is art, the hidden logic. No creative writer is satisfied with the limits of coherent thought. He speaks without knowing what he will say, and it is because he does not know that he is forced to speak, since art is discovery. The apparently chaotic surface of modern art presents naturalistically an environment filled with objects which cannot be conceptually connected, for the fringes of nature seem like this to our limited perception. Bold manipulation of material is a quest for the right language, beyond sense, non-sensical. And even Chandos, silent now, feels that there must be a language in which he may think and speak coherently, not English or Italian or any of the habitual forms, but a new language, a total language, 'a language, not even one of whose words is known to me, a language in which the mute things speak to me and in which I shall one day, in the grave, perhaps justify myself to an unknown judge'. This unknown judge presides over Kafka's court too, the father who is form, the spur to effort, approachable only through 'the mute things', which are the mysterious phenomena of the world about us, objects and events whose vibrations must be transcribed into the connective language of art.

Chandos is idle, he lives a life of 'hardly credible emptiness'; and he is idle because he despairs of language, his sole access to form. But his idleness is the cause as well as effect of his despair. All transformation is work, and without work there can be no transformation, which is change in the stream of energy as it flows from the known to the unknown. Chandos is lost in a nameless ocean of experience. He almost knows, almost. But the right name, the magic name, eludes him. Yet he can justify himself only by discovering the right name. How else can he transform this straw of life into gold? It is tantalizing; literally, for his fate reminds him of that other punishment: 'How can I attempt to portray these strange spiritual torments to you, this sudden raising of the fruit above my outstretched hands, this retreat of the murmuring water from my thirsting lips?'

Chandos the poet knows all about the fate of Tantalus. He too has been close to the gods and is now fallen from the Parnassus of harmony into a living grave—as Adam falls into self-consciousness, as Icarus falls from rivalry with the sun, as Mephistopheles falls from the ranks of the angels. Always the dual principle of divine and devilish, perfect god and fragmented human, tree of life and flaming sword, as the serpent too is both sinister and friendly, tempter and also symbol of knowledge and healing, associated with Apollo and the rod of Aesculapius. Man likes to have it both ways in the imaginative visions of myth, since the darkness through which he gropes, feeling and forming his way, is not only present torment but also the only avenue to knowledge. But does this dualism exist anywhere but in the human mind? Attributing exceptional powers to the gods is our way of blaming the universe for our mistakes. It is hell which justifies humanity and gives it the will to live.

Goethe and the Historic Moment

Nature makes no convenient exceptions for man. Perhaps this knowledge is the prime aspect of human genius, which is rare because it is natural. Hedged in by habit, we deny our potential. Imagination is the free pursuit of all the possibilities inherent in a situation. This is everybody's potential, but only the genius is equipped for such freedom. He can and must follow the possibilities, wherever they may lead.

The free pursuit of latent possibilities is also the process of natural growth. This means transformation, as one form succeeds another, perhaps changed utterly, but joined, as leaf is joined to seed. But there exists (in the sense of having immediate life) only one stage in transformation. This is the present surface, accessible to eye and ear and hand, the surface here now, product of its past and sole origin of its future. In art too we meet the present surface, no more, a static image of the fluid moment. This static image is true when charged with possibilities. The stillness of the work of art is an illusion, like the apparent stillness of form in nature.

Goethe tells us in a late poem that only the fruitful thing is really true. His own pursuit of fruitful development began early, and continued. Always the emphasis on continuity and change. When he was twenty-one and a law student at Strasbourg he gave this advice to a friend who wrote to him about future studies: 'We must *be* nothing, but desire to *become* everything, and especially not stand still longer than the requirements of a tired mind and body demand.' Sixty years later the same principle ruled his existence. 'A man must change constantly,' he now said, 'renew himself, rejuvenate himself, so as not to harden into a mould.' The astonishing variety of his activities throughout this long life makes the unity of his vision all the more impressive, and convincing.

Goethe never remained the same, except as the leaf is the seed. This is how he wanted to develop, fruitfully, truthfully, growing like a natural object through a succession of vital moments, finding his own future on the basis of the present, this surface at hand, which he called the historic moment. 'We learn to value the moment', he said, 'as soon as we make it historic.' This means realizing its potential, and its potential is history.

The historic moment is the present situation, which is all that we have, seen as a stage in transformation, the only point from which the future can emerge, the point from which it must emerge as an organic possibility. A visitor to the great man at Weimar told him he had seen nothing of significance on his travels. Goethe replied: 'There is nothing insignificant in the world. It all depends how you look at things.'

Goethe knew how to look at things. There is only one way for the genius—openly, without prejudice. On the day he arrived at Strasbourg as a student he saw the Gothic cathedral. The conventional taste of his time held that Gothic was a barbaric mode, its style no style at all but a formless extravagance of random detail. Goethe did not share the conventional taste of his time, or of any time. He was a poet, he was interested in truth, he looked for what was there, not for what he would have liked to see there.

This poet, already a scientist in attitude, allowed the object before him to make its impression—and the impression was ecstasy. These pillars thrusting into the sky were, he said, trees of God. The twists of Gothic ornament at the periphery sprang from the centre like leaves from the tree. This great work of art was true because it was fruitful. Each aspect seemed an organic development, connected and continuous, characteristic of its source, as the historic moment, the surface at hand, is always shaped by the character of its past. Goethe now spoke of 'characteristic art', which he described as the only true art. By this term he meant the static image seen as a stage in transformation, its form characterized by its past history and pointing to its future development. Everything flows.

So the apparent disorder of Gothic is seen as pattern, a design of organic stages in space, equivalent to that succession of living moments which is the process of growth. This is the visible present, all that we have. But what of the future, waiting to emerge and become in its turn the historic moment?

Goethe's ecstasy at Strasbourg came from a magical sense of identity with the observed object. In this state of intuitive understanding he was able to go further. His surrender to organic forces meant he could enter the life of the structure before him and pursue its possibilities to a stage it had not yet reached. Imagination is necessarily based on experience, but goes beyond experience. Even the lunatic's visions of horror, as William James remarked, are drawn from the material of daily fact.

When Goethe wrote about this Strasbourg experience he went on from his appreciation of the building as an organic unity to outline the unknown (because unrealized) intentions of the medieval architect. Nobody knew then what the plans had been, but later the original drawings were found, and Goethe's suppositions were now seen to be true. He found the truth because his process was true, and his process was the free pursuit of the possibilities inherent in this situation, the cathedral. This is like the poet's imaginative creation of an image. The most persuasive feature of any real work of art is that its shape seems inevitable. We perform the miracle of recognizing what we have never seen before, and we recognize it because it is characteristic of its source. It surprises us but confirms our expectations.

Goethe described his writings as fragments of a great confession. It would be interesting to speculate how many novels

are really disguised warnings from the author to himself.
Goethe put on the mask of fiction to tell the truth about his
fears. His first novel, *The Sorrows of Young Werther*, is about a
man who fails because he will not accept the principle which
governs life, as it governed Goethe's existence: the principle of
constant change and development.

At first, Werther's condition is a state of ecstasy, like Goethe's
before the cathedral. Werther too is looking at an organic
construction, this time nature itself, and feeling intuitive
identity with it. The complexity of natural forms serves only
to increase his wonder and joy, for this peripheral variety
speaks to him of a resolute organic centre. The whole world is
a harmony in which he himself is rapturously embedded. His
error is that he attributes his joy to a particular state and not to
a specific process. He cannot imagine any happier condition, so
he wants to switch off the possibilities of change, he wants to
freeze the state of bliss and make the present moment last for
ever. If nature will not co-operate by checking the constant
flow, he will insist on his right as a human being to be an
exception to natural law.

As Goethe said, it all depends how you look at things.
Werther finds that the friendly face of nature has now changed
and become hostile. Everything is in conflict. The peripheral
details are suddenly separate and confusing. But nature is no
different. It is Werther's interpretation which has changed.
He looks for what he wants to find there, he looks for the convenient exception which does not exist. Harmony springs
apart. The immense complexities which once seemed so
securely locked together now become disconnected fragments,
and Werther is one of them, a particle among particles, a
meaningless object tumbling in a disintegrated world. The
modern theme of alienation is here, in this eighteenth-century
novel.

In his despair Werther recalls the image of the crucifixion of
Christ and repeats those final words: 'My God, my God, why
have you forsaken me?' It is as though the smiling face of

harmony, which is authority beyond explanation, has been capriciously withdrawn. Werther is human to the last. He looks for a scapegoat. It is not his fault; the blame obviously lies in a world whose harmony now escapes him. This is why he complains that his past joy and his present misery both spring from the same source. But he deludes himself. He thinks the source is outside himself, when it is within. Nature is indifferent. It is not nature which has a dual face, it is Werther. He could once accept the organic process of life and be happy; he must now deny the fundamental requirement of nature— that life be in flux, a succession of vital moments.

Werther fails because he will not accept the moment as historic. He does not wish to pursue its possibilities into the future. This denial is human, and the source of human isolation, Werther's last stand, with the whole of nature out of step and apparently out of sympathy. Such human presumption is the sin against the holy ghost, because it stands in opposition to the essence of life. It is the crime whose possibility also lurks at the centre of Goethe's *Faust*.

In Goethe's play, Faust is the man who wants to see how everything hangs together. He starts from the other extreme: he is not in ecstasy, he is a cold observer of detached phenomena. It is easy to observe a particular event; the difficulty comes when we must relate this to a universal arrangement, since our experience is not formed by universal arrangements but only by particular events, the facts of our perception. Faust wants to know truth. He exposes himself to the apparent chaos of detail in his world so that he may realize the universal in the only possible way—by accepting the particular and pursuing its possibilities.

Faust's pact with the devil is not the naïve bargain of 'You serve me in this world, and I'll serve you in the next'. This arrangement would have satisfied Mephistopheles (he is not a particularly imaginative demon), but Faust is working for eternity. He complicates the contract by imposing another condition, not on the devil but on himself. He says that if he should ever wish the passing moment to stay for ever, he will give up life and follow Mephistopheles to hell. Does he have the fate of Werther in mind? For he is referring to the essential condition for all life, not merely his own. To deny flux is to deny life, which is the fluid pursuit of possibilities through a succession of historic moments. The pact is with himself. Either he accepts life for what it is, or he gives it up. There will be no need for the devil to *take* him. To place a finite human term on the moment is to join the devil, who is defined in this play as 'the spirit which always denies'.

Man has the choice between transformation or guilt. Denial is not in the world, it is in man. This is the meaning of Faust's promise to Mephistopheles, the devil waiting within. Werther found it convenient to blame his isolation on the hostility of a world he had denied. Faust is wiser: he knows, as Werther does not, that the danger is in himself, not in the world. When Goethe became a Minister in the small state of Weimar the Duke asked him to draw up the fire regulations. He must have assessed his resident poet pretty shrewdly. What else had Goethe been doing all his life?

At Weimar Goethe began his serious studies in natural science. There was no conflict with the poet. These studies were an extension of his poetic faculty. 'Fabrication out of thin air', said Goethe, 'was never my method. I have always regarded the world as more gifted with genius than I.' This world, he believed, would come to him if he opened himself to it. His curiosity and keen visual sense drew him as readily to the observation of plants and rocks and bones as to the observation of cathedrals. Take things as they are, not as we might wish them to be: this was, for Goethe, a guiding principle. The impact of particular events was of supreme importance, since each event was a historic moment, its character shaped organically and producing an organic shape. It was true because charged with possibilities, gifted with genius.

In 1792 Duke Karl-August of Weimar commanded a Prussian regiment in the combined force which moved against the French. Goethe went with him on the campaign. His journal reveals his sense of priorities. During the bombardment of Verdun his interest was focused on the prismatic effects of sunlight glancing on small fish in a crater filled with water. He experimented by throwing bits of earthenware into the water and was pleased to note that the results confirmed his initial impressions.

That night, as the heavy bombardment continued, he walked up and down in the open air with Prince Reuss. Their conversation continued until dawn. Goethe spoke of his colour theories, recalled by the afternoon's experience of refraction. When he came to write his journal he remarked, of the fish and of light: 'My experience with these evolutions of natural phenomena was like my experience with poems: I did not make them, they made me.'

At the battle of Valmy he looked objectively at the reactions of the human body to heavy gunfire, the body in this experiment being his own. Friendly officers warned him he was risking his life. To them he must have seemed utterly remote from the realities of the day, but this opinion simply placed him in the long tradition of divine fools who seem aloof, perhaps stupid, because they are integrated in a life larger than the vainly human segment.

On this day, at Valmy, the Prussians of the old Europe capitulated before the revolutionary defiance of the new. It was the man who seemed most remote from the realities of the day who saw the consequences of this failure more clearly than anyone. That night Goethe stood in a circle of disconsolate men. He was asked his opinion of the day's events. He said: 'From here and now a new epoch in world history begins, and you can say you were present at its birth.'

The masses were on the move. One world of privilege was coming to an end. It was a period of change, so upsetting to man but so natural to *this* man, for whom change had always been a governing principle of existence. As a historic moment, Valmy was no exceptional experience for Goethe. The scientist-poet merely did what he always did—he observed precisely what was before his eyes, and he pursued the latent possibilities freely. To continue the development of Valmy into the future was like sensing the missing but inevitable fragments of Strasbourg.

This is transformation, the present becoming the future, changed but joined, visible only and always as an immediate surface, the historic present. Goethe believed the only fruitful course for man is co-operation with a world gifted with genius. He immersed himself in this world and respected its processes.

In a letter only a few days before his death in 1832, he said: 'The best kind of talent is that which absorbs everything into itself and can appropriate everything without letting it do the slightest injury to its own peculiar basic quality, its character.' And, looking back on his long life, perhaps thinking of the tremendous variety of his experience, the many so-called 'opposites' united in his work, he said to a friend: 'What have I achieved? Everything I have seen, heard and observed, I have used. My works have been fed by countless different individuals . . . by ignoramuses and wise men, by intellectuals and by idiots. Childhood, middle age, old age—all have offered me their thoughts, their capabilities, their hopes and their views on life. I have often harvested what others have sown. My work is the work of a collective being who bears the name Goethe.'

Wave-grain in the Wall

Stone is the most expressive material. It is a frozen sea grained with waves. Or a magnetic field of particles suspended in pattern. It is evidence of form and memory of movement, a memory which awakens in the imaginative observer. Movement is its essential and secret quality: in legend water springs from the rock, reminding us that the miraculous is the commonplace we have forgotten. 'If you look at some old wall covered with dirt', says Leonardo in his *Treatise on Painting*, 'or the odd appearance of some streaked stones, you may discover several things like landscapes, battles, clouds, uncommon attitudes, humorous faces, draperies, and so on. Out of this confused mass of objects the mind will be furnished with abundance of designs and subjects, perfectly new.'

The hero of Robert Musil's novel *Young Törless* is a pupil at a boarding-school in the country. He has a strange experience one day. He has gone out into the park; he lies down in the grass under the wall of the school building, doing nothing in particular, looking up at the sky; and suddenly, through a hole in the clouds, he sees infinity.

He knows the word. He has used it in mathematics. He has used it in calculations as a definite quantity; and if you can calculate with a concept it is under control, friendly, comforting. But 'infinity' is not friendly now, in nature. It is not definite. It goes on and on through that hole in the clouds, endless, beyond thought, beyond any definition he knows. He feels as if some animal tamed in his schoolroom concept has suddenly slipped its chain and become savage again. It threatens him. Something wild and destructive, sleeping in that convenient mathematical term, has now awakened. It has, of course, awakened in Törless, in his sharpened perceptions; 'awakened', he says, 'and become fruitful again.'

It is Törless himself who describes this experience as both destructive and fruitful. Is destruction the same as creation? What has happened to him is that the familiar barrier of definition has collapsed; he realizes that human concepts are inadequate as an image of experience. They do not go far enough. There is more, there is knowledge beyond thought. It is there now, in the sky, real but intangible—because his words cannot define it. And not only in the sky: this immediate experience in the grass represents a larger crisis of sensibility. People and all the things around him are seen in a new light. Or a new darkness, since the deeper experience which flows over him is accessible only to feeling; so it is vague, puzzling, a world of shadows. Here, he senses, are concealed the connections which will explain everything that seems contradictory in life.

For his life is confused; and his confusion comes from apparent contradiction between labels, between order and disorder, between the acceptable and the unacceptable which is also present and real. Explanation is simply connection. Without connection there is no understanding. Törless, like everybody else, wants to understand, but he sees no logical connection, only a mysterious one. Schopenhauer remarks that all learning and all knowledge depend on the inexplicable. Kafka retells the story of Prometheus and comes to the conclusion that legend is an attempt to explain the inexplicable. In this sense, all his stories are legends. 'Since legend rests on a foundation of truth,' says Kafka, 'it must end again in the inexplicable.' Truth is more than logic. The hidden connection between forms, the unseen causality, is the foundation of truth.

Törless now rests in this inexplicable world. His experience of infinity seems destructive because it shatters accepted explanation and so threatens every formal arrangement in his life; it is also fruitful (potentially, at least) because growth comes only when formal arrangement is fluid arrangement. Destruction is change of structure, not elimination. The constituents of form are never destroyed; they are rearranged, they re-form in new associations. This is natural transformation, the fruit of destruction.

Musil began his novel only a year or so after Hofmannsthal spoke in his 'Chandos Letter' about the writer's despair of language. Hofmannsthal too described the moment when feeling understands more than concept can offer, and therefore more than known language (which is definition of concept) can express. The theme of this letter is that there *is* knowledge beyond human knowledge. The scale of values which determines everyday response to experience is a relative judgement based on accepted knowledge. When this knowledge is seen to be limited and therefore inadequate, the scale of values crumbles.

What happens to the individual in this situation is that he finds he has based his judgement up to now on insufficient evidence. The case is reopened, without prejudice. And, where there is no prejudice, *all* the evidence is equally important. For Hofmannsthal's Chandos a beetle swimming in a bucket of water can be the whole world, filling his mind with meaning. This is vision—seeing the invisible but eternal coherence of all things. But how to express this meaning? Words fail him. They do not go this far.

Törless also relates the perplexing vagueness of his experience of infinity to the inadequacy of known language. Musil puts it like this: 'It was a refusal of words which tormented him there, a half-awareness that words are only chance refuges for what is felt.' Törless, lying in the grass, is surrounded by mute things which fascinate and confuse. Everything within the range of his senses is important and charged with meaning. The grey wall of the school seems to bend over him and look down at him. A rustling sound comes to him from the stones. A strange life, we are told, awakens in the wall. It is like the strange life which has awakened in the sleeping concept 'infinity'—strange, inexplic-

able, urgent. These stones speak, but in a language Törless is
not tuned to understand. It is impossible for him to understand.
He is now experiencing the fertile combination of conscious
and unconscious, so the essence of understanding lies outside his
rational mind. It is like the world of legend where feeling seems
concrete yet hovers beyond explicit understanding, because the
foundation of truth rests in the dark unconscious.

In legend the god can be stone or beetle or swan. For Törless
the wall can be the whole of experience, as every object can
contain the whole of meaning. But objects can be repulsive as
well as fascinating. Where is the eternal coherence in apparent
evil? The events which confuse Törless are mainly concerned
with a prostitute and a thieving schoolboy from the same class
at school as well as social class, so someone very near him. What
is the connection, he asks, between the prostitute and his
mother? What is the connection between the thief and himself?
The prostitute exists, the thief exists. Without connection there
is simply no sense. But connection here is obscene. Are the
daylight world and the dark really separate from each other? If
so, there is no meaning to the life he now experiences, only a
selective social meaning which describes the dark as immoral.
This, for Törless, is a one-sided meaning—and that is no meaning at all. He is looking for the explanation behind unspeakable
impulses, not for an alibi.

The idea of evil is our alibi. The devil is a convenient waste-
paper basket for everything excluded from our concept of
good. Excluded but still there in that useful phantom, because
it is still there in the world. His very existence is an acknowledgement that moral education is selective. But Törless is no
longer selective. The dark is as real to him as the moral world
of his parents. It is not only the concept of infinity which now
loses its firm outline and becomes destructive and fruitful.
Every concept, even the concept of good, dissolves into fluid
possibilities. 'Everything happens,' says Törless; 'this is the
whole of wisdom.' It is a dangerous wisdom. Only the saint
can afford to ignore the rules of virtue.

Törless now digs into the dark side of life which has been concealed from him under moral prohibition. He digs into it because he senses that here he will find truth, because truth is total or it is nothing. All aspects of life contribute to it. And this is why Kafka's images are so often dark and distracting and foul. They project his experience of a world which is at the same time fascinating and confusing, intangibly true and precisely horrible. It is the inexplicable which must be understood; the rest is partial and therefore unsatisfactory. Kafka's novels are pictures of experience as it falls on the author's open sensibility, accepted for what it is and probed without prejudice. The court of judgement is everywhere because it is the constant puzzle of existence.

In *The Trial* Joseph K. goes to see the painter Titorelli. He hopes Titorelli may be able to help him in his struggle with the unseen court where *his* unknown judge presides. The truth is always out of sight, a dark expectation. But in Kafka approximation to truth is always approximation to darkness, real physical darkness; his heroes now stumble across obstacles and events from the rejected world, things which the human scale of values must classify as unclean or immoral.

When Joseph K. comes to the place where Titorelli lives, he finds the houses dark, the alleys littered with filth. Then he comes to the wall. It is the wall of the painter's house, near the door. A hole has been broken through at the bottom, and from this hole, 'as K. approached'—and I think it is important that Kafka says this: it is as though all the pulses of life in the narrative are pulses of K.'s life, and the events his mental state given form, his own reaction to experience—at this moment a repulsive yellow, reeking fluid shoots out of the hole. Rats run before it into the neighbouring canal. A deafening din bursts from the workshop next door, for the distracting surface of life assaults all the senses, not merely the sense of sight. Is this hole like Törless's hole in the clouds—endless, threatening, but tantalizingly significant and full of promise? This, for K., is the access to Titorelli, the hope of truth.

If the road to truth lies through such horrors it can also be the road to madness. What if form never comes? In a world without concepts and their associated scale of values there is no apparent order. How can the human personality survive without the punctuation of values and classification? The scale of values defends and protects. The whole point of moral education is that it is a defensive exercise.

Hermann Hesse's novel *Steppenwolf* examines the same road and acknowledges explicitly that it is a possible road to madness. Harry Haller is part man, part wolf. Not really wolf, of course; the wolf is a legend for that part of him which rejects social values and therefore lives like a wild animal in the dark, the dark of the unconscious and the unknown, where he too senses truth to lie. This dark region seems destructive to society but fruitful to Haller.

He walks alone through an old town one night, in the rain. He thinks about past experience and remembers particularly some music heard at a concert which gave him a sudden vision of wholeness, of the divine, like a track of gold (he says) running through all things. And he does mean all things—no exclusions, no human reservations, no polite judgements. This is what he says: 'I dropped all my defences and was afraid of nothing in the world. I accepted all things, and to all things I gave up my heart.'

As he walks on he comes to the inevitable wall. Here again it stands like a legend, inexplicable, both obstacle and access to truth. It is the image of his experience. He now sees with some surprise (he doesn't remember noticing this before) that there is a small door in the wall. He has not seen it before because experience does not always offer access; that sense of revelation in the distracting wall of daily events is occasional. There seems to be an electric sign over the door. He can't read it at first. It flashes fitfully and faintly, even vanishes at times, like vision itself, that sudden vision in the dark which, like the poet's inspiration, cannot be willed.

At last he manages to make out several words. 'Magic

Theatre. Entrance not for Everybody.' He tries to open the door, but he can't. He turns away, and now he sees coloured letters reflected on the wet road, and he reads: 'For Madmen Only.' And immediately he recalls that earlier occasional vision of wholeness which he calls the divine, or the track of gold. 'A fragment of my former thoughts came suddenly to my mind, the similarity to the track of shining gold which is again so suddenly remote and cannot be found.' The door in the wall, with its wavering electric sign, affects him like music. What he sees is the divine in all things, stone, beetle, or cloud, equally enchanting in the magic theatre of experience. The track of gold exists in the daily wall of experienced obstacles. But he has been warned. This road of total acceptance is for madmen only.

Rilke speaks in his prose work *The Notebook of Malte Laurids Brigge* about what he calls 'the existence of the terrible in every particle of the air'. The theme at this point is: no selection, no rejection. Truth is total, so everything matters and must be faced, however offensive it may appear to human senses. 'It seems to me', says Rilke through his young hero Malte, 'as if this were the decisive thing: whether you could persuade yourself to lie down with the leper and warm him with the heart-warmth of nights of love; only good can come of that.'

This is Harry Haller's complete acceptance in the face of insanity, Joseph K.'s progress through the apparently repulsive, Törless's compelling curiosity about prostitute and thief. They act as they do from the conviction that only good can come of that. Their surroundings are both source of distraction and of truth, both obstacle and access.

In Rilke's book Malte is a young Dane who lives in Paris. He has the poet's curiosity about experience. He has the poet's immense and necessary boldness. Is it possible, he wonders, that after thousands of years of human history nothing real and important has yet been seen or known or said? 'Is it possible that in spite of discoveries and progress, in spite of culture, religion, and secular wisdom, we have remained on the surface of life?' 'Is it possible that all realities are nothing to people,

that their life ticks away, unconnected with anything, like a
clock in an empty room?' Malte believes all these things are
possible. He resolves to sit in his room on the fifth floor and
write. From this empty room he will seek connections, assert
his part in what has been hidden up to now, as if he is the first
man to see and know and utter. He will write day and night.
And he writes about a wall.

It is the last surviving wall of some demolished houses. It
fascinates him. It fills his mind and soul, and in fact it is his
mind and soul, perception given form.

He describes the wall. He is looking at the inner side.
Memories of rooms are marked by scraps of wallpaper and
fragments of beams. The rusty channel of a lavatory pipe coils
down like some disgusting digestive tract. Malte's description
probes every sickening detail, because every detail matters:
reality is everything and every thing is real. His picture is one of
decay and filth. The leper has taken shape. And from visible
corruption Malte moves to the invisible life of the past, which
is always present. The breath of the many lives spent in these
rooms comes over him. 'There were the midday meals and
sicknesses and the exhaled breath and the smoke of years and
the sweat which breaks out under armpits and makes the
clothes heavy, and stale breath from mouths and the oily
smell of swollen feet. There was the sharp tang of urine and
burning soot and the grey vapour of potatoes and the heavy,
sickly stench of rancid grease.'

No selection, no rejection. This is Malte's way of lying down
with the leper, believing only good can come of that. But it is
not the human concept of good as we have known it up to
now. The devil is here too, and madness. Malte welcomes and
embraces everything. It happens. It is there, so it must have
meaning. The wall is his experience and he recognizes it; this is
why it is both fearful and fascinating to him, repulsive and
compelling. He ends the episode of the wall like this: 'But I've
said (haven't I?) that all the walls had been demolished except
the last one. Now it's of this wall that I've been talking all

along. You will say I must have stood a long time in front of it, but I'll swear an oath I began to run as soon as I recognized the wall. For the frightful thing is that I did recognize it. I recognize everything here; that's why it penetrates me immediately. It is at home in me.'

The wall is at home in Törless and Harry Haller and Joseph K. too. This is what they see in themselves, this abundance of designs and subjects. They are not struggling with an exterior world. They are listening for the language of connection in a world which can only be at home in them. The wall speaks to them as clearly and as mysteriously as a face seen in a mirror, where the image of profound identity is surface and only surface, an inexplicable legend.

Cordelia and the Button

THERE must have been more important things in my army career than buttons on the back of a greatcoat. But this is what I remember: a sea-front in south Wales, deserted in winter; we'd come out for morning roll-call, and there we stood, in ranks, waiting. Perhaps I was bored or cold. I suddenly became aware of the buttons on the back of a greatcoat in front of me.

How do we become aware? Is there an urgency of vibrations which cry to us for no logical reason? Buttons. Why not the sea, curlews, the importantly poetical things? These were urgent in their time, but not now. For some magical reason and for a few seconds the buttons on that khaki cloth, their shape, the fall of light on patterned brass, the curve of shadow —this was meaning which I could not define.

And this is magic: an effect whose cause we can't see. But that's the definition of absurdity too—an effect whose cause we can't see—except that in absurdity it's a cause we can't believe in either. For magic we do have a secret belief, and this belief spans that gap between cause and effect. A button is a button. How then can it be more, charged with meaning like the Book of Common Prayer, whose words made my colourful Sunday on church parade? Hopkins asks that we praise 'all trades, their gear and tackle and trim'. It's not only in fairy-tales that buttons are surprising and potent. I discovered this on that sea-front and knew there was a rainbow connection between that plain shape and what I jokingly call my immortal soul.

Poetry postulates the hidden connection. Goethe tells us that without poetry nothing works. By poetry he means all art, all imaginative extension. Art begins from what we know and projects from there, the white light becomes impossibly coloured, the rainbow. We see how things work when we see how the parts are connected and how they act on each other. This is what Goethe means: art makes those connections which give meaning to our experience, connections we don't normally see. Poetry gives probability to the disjointed world.

Poetry, according to Goethe, is fairy-tale. Does he contradict himself? For surely, if poetry is fairy-tale, this leads us away from probability and into a disjointed world. The characteristic of fairy-tale or tale of magic, the *Märchen*, is that objects and people are placed in apparently impossible juxtaposition: frog and prince, pumpkin and coach. Goethe describes poetry as fairy-tale because in both the elements may seem disconnected yet are invisibly joined through transformation. Connections are not stated, but the process of transformation implies them. It is the same in nature: there are connections we don't normally see. The quivering cell in nature is like the isolated fact in poetry and fairy-tale. It is vitally itself and urgently something more, the word which opens out.

We experience *things*. We don't experience infinity, we don't experience the universal. We have no sense-organs for these. All things fall on us as vibrations, as facts. This is the physical basis of poetry as fairy-tale. In both it is the fact which is presented to us, as the fact is presented in daily experience, the fact which is fluid, ready for development. The universal and the apparently infinite can consist only of the present fact taken further. Poetry makes its impact by suggesting the future while remaining in the present. It implies the universal by keeping to the particular.

My buttons were poetry, a particular shape pregnant with possibilities. Once we escape from definitions and stop putting ideas before experience, then all trades, their gear and tackle and trim, become poetry, the fairy-tale in action, no different from grained leaf, contoured stone, face and hat and snail-shell.

Modern art specializes in the isolated object presented in impossible conjunction. Is this absurdity? Or is it magic? It is the method of the fairy-tale. There is a sense (perhaps the only sense) in which 'originality' means 'a return to our origins'. We have gone back to the primitive tale of magic.

The Welsh poet Taliesin lived in north Britain in the sixth century. A medieval manuscript tells about the circumstances of his birth. It is a tale of magic, poetry about the birth of poetry. The historical person and historical time are lost in legend, as impossible and as haunting as the legend of the unicorn.

The story begins with Ceridwen, a noblewoman living in north Wales at the time of King Arthur. She has two children. Her daughter is beautiful, the boy is the ugliest creature on earth. Ceridwen decides she must give him some admirable quality to compensate for his ugliness. She will give him supreme intelligence, not just sharpness of wit but total knowledge.

She consults the magic books and follows their instructions. A cauldron of herbs has to simmer over the fire for a year and a day. She learns from the books which herbs to gather. They must be collected and added to the brew at different seasons, with due regard to the position of the planets. Ceridwen is out and about during this year and a day, she has no time to stir the cauldron and tend the fire. For these trivial tasks she employs an insignificant peasant boy from the locality. Is anything trivial? Is any object insignificant? Ceridwen knows a lot, but she hasn't studied poetry.

The peasant boy is called Gwion. He stirs the cauldron, he tends the fire. Ceridwen comes and goes. At last the time is up, all herbs added, the brew now effective. Ceridwen comes to collect her work and use it for her purpose. As she comes in through the door three drops fly out of the cauldron and fall by accident on Gwion's hand. Are there any accidents? J. M. W. Turner is supposed to have said: 'I never lose an accident.' The accident too is magic: it is an event whose causation we cannot

G

see. The cauldron splits in two. Ceridwen sees her work destroyed; she rushes for Gwion, meaning to kill him.

Now it is Gwion who has supreme knowledge. The brew really works. It works as poetry works. Everything that follows tells us that supreme knowledge is perception of the unity of all life. There is no separation, no fixed form, only interconnection as one shape melts into another.

The form which is Gwion changes into the form of a hare. He runs from the wrath of this stumbling human. But she is a student of magic, she too knows about invisible connections. She transforms herself to match his transformation. She becomes a greyhound which streaks after its natural prey. She is about to catch it and kill it when the hare leaps into the river and swims away, now a fish at home in its element, seemingly safe from the dog behind it. But the dog isn't there. Instead, an otter drives through the water in pursuit of the fish, equally at home in the river and swifter and stronger. Gwion escapes by leaving the water and entering the third element, the air. He is now a bird. He flies up into freedom. But above him waits the hawk, Ceridwen, shadowing him, preparing to strike. There seems no escape this time. She silently falls to kill. The bird is no longer there. Gwion is a grain of corn which drifts to earth and comes to rest on the floor of a barn, a single grain lost in a multitude of grains. This is infinity, the confusing mass which is however not infinite to complete perception but a collection of finite and particular grains. There on the threshing floor is a black hen which scratches and searches and eventually finds and swallows the grain which is Gwion.

Is this life then eliminated? Everything flows. The form changes, the end is a beginning, our words define the indefinable. When Ceridwen returns to human shape she finds she is pregnant. Nine months later she gives birth to a son, so beautiful she hasn't the heart to kill him. Life is insistent. 'So she wrapped him in a leathern bag, and cast him into the sea to the mercy of God, on the twenty-ninth day of April.'

The date is precise. A fact is a fact. This is the particular event which is, like all events, like all objects, like my buttons even, rooted in its own context of time and place. The event changes, form moves on, but in each moment, at each stage, the cellular arrangement is exact. There is nothing vague about life, except our contemplation of it. Art persuades us that the impossible is inevitable. It does so, in Breughel and in Bosch, in Gogol and in Kafka, by giving precise delineation to the fantastical, by accepting the extraordinary as a logical extension of the ordinary. Brecht always had above his desk a notice which said: 'The truth is concrete.' Perhaps he had to be reminded. We all have to be reminded.

So the child is cast into the sea to the mercy of God. He is found. If you are cast adrift in a folk-tale you can be sure you will be carried, and preserved, on the stream of transformation. The currents may be unseen, but they are certain. They connect what seems disconnected. This is the realm in which you never lose an accident, the fairy-tale which is poetry, the home of concealed logic. The child moves in the sea as all life moves and develops, its future latent in its present. What more appropriate region for transformation than the sea? The leathern bag is caught in a fisherman's net, the child emerges from the sea, he rises like Venus from the sea, our origins, the fact and image of fluidity *and* fertility.

When Goethe described his return from Leipzig to his home in Frankfurt as a young student, he said he went back there 'like a shipwrecked man'. This sense of having just stumbled ashore stayed with him. When he was thirty he noted in his diary that even now, with (as he thought) half his life behind him, he seemed to have done nothing, achieved nothing, made no firm path for himself, but to be standing there like a man who has just crawled out of the water. This is the perpetual beginning, the present moment, the moment in which we are always saving ourselves from drowning. The past is fluid, the present flows into the future, any sense of firm ground is illusory because growth is movement. The emergence of the child from the sea is true because it is this moment which is every moment, changing, powerfully potential, elusive but precise. The child found in the fisherman's net is given a name, a new name, for the new shape is a new thing and therefore a new word, which stands for the thing itself. He is called Taliesin.

Gwion has gone through the nine-month cycle of human transformation, in which fluid becomes form (but an ever-changing form). Now, with the radiant pedigree of partheno-genesis, the mercy of God and the fruitful sea, he finds himself translated into Taliesin, the divine singer. For Taliesin is a poet. The historical Taliesin has somehow merged into this mythical figure who is both god and poet, a kind of Welsh Orpheus.

The story of Orpheus and the story of Taliesin share the same philosophical substance. In both, art is associated with magic. Both are about transformation (which is only the essential flow and development of every form). In both there is power over nature, acquaintance with death, emergence of life from the grave, spring from winter. For Taliesin the grave is literally the womb of life, as he is carried by Ceridwen in the dark. Afterwards the sea is the second tomb, in which nothing dies, and from which the god is resurrected.

What we have is a story which represents the unity of life and affirms the belief that all forms in our environment are con-nected and continuous. It is worth noting that the magic begins with what we know, Gwion the boy doing what we have all done at times . . . stirring the pot. (When I first wrote that phrase, my perverse typewriter said 'stirring the poet', and for some reason it said it the second time too, so perhaps I should have left it at that, on the principle of never losing an accident.)

Infinity is the finite, extended. Poetry does begin from the commonplace. There is no other beginning. This is the per-petual beginning, the child emerging from the sea, the human form surrounded by the water of experience which is its home and only sustenance. Not only the human form. Every form is the transitory and indivisible phenomenon which represents the past and promises the future.

This expression 'indivisible phenomenon' comes from Goethe. He uses it to point exactly to the object, the event, which we should accept for what it is, a union of cause and effect, productive from this moment on. 'The thinking man', says Goethe, 'makes a particular mistake when he inquires about cause and effect. Both together make the indivisible phenomenon. The man who realizes this is on the right road to action, to the deed.'

When Goethe speaks of art as fairy-tale he means that both work with forms as indivisible phenomena, forms whose connecting links cannot be seen. 'I don't draw people,' says Kafka, 'I tell stories.' That is, he doesn't describe, explain, analyse. He presents facts, as nature does no more than present facts. This is the telling of stories, the utterance, the expression, an arrangement of forms, as the story of Taliesin is an arrangement of forms without explanatory links.

Great imagination is never abstract. It follows the procedure of art and is the procedure of art, as it is the course of nature and the face of fairy-tale. It takes the fact of the present moment and develops it into another shape, as tangible and as potent.

Shakespeare's *Lear* ends in a cosmic storm of feeling. The old king with dead Cordelia in his arms. Is this the image of horror? We hear the words which are the news and philosophy of grief. 'Why should a dog, a horse, a rat, have life, and thou no breath at all?' But somehow this remains philosophy, something thought up, a gloss, a description. The lightning flash comes with a moment which seems irrelevant because apparently isolated from the action, accidental. It comes when Lear, in his tumult of grief, turns to his companions and says: 'Pray you, undo this button.' From the mist of philosophy emerges the human figure, stark, alone. Here is the exact isolation of agony, majestic on a level we can all understand, the level of a button which has become an indivisible phenomenon. All poetry and majesty and grief and hope are here. Art is not about abstractions or ultimate issues or infinity or eternity. Art is about buttons.

Animals of Silence

ADAPT your form to the job in hand. This seems to be a basic principle of natural development and of folk-tale. If one form is not suitable, try another. The branches of a tree grow and shift and shape themselves according to the necessities of light and weather, conforming to pressures. Not being eliminated by pressures but maintaining their own characteristics in agreement with other forces.

We know how people too can take on the right shape for the job. An uncle of mine was a shepherd on the Welsh mountains. He spent his whole life up there. The place shaped him into the man he was. His back was hunched round his head. He didn't seem to have a neck, his chin touched his chest like a beard. He didn't so much stand on the earth as emerge from it, as if only what was rooted would endure in that place and that weather. When he stood on the bare slope he looked like a blunt rock cropped out of the earth, or a thorn tree bent back into itself. From a distance indeed, in those hills, what was he? Rock? Tree? Man? It was hard to tell. What I remember best about him is his expressive shape—and his expressive silence. Nature does not speak with the language of men. It seems that man too, as he approaches a natural state, relies more on silence than on the words of human language.

The normal changes of growth and adaptation do not strike us as transformation. We still see the basic shape, the same language of bark and leaves and branches. A man has suddenly to put on a wig before we can say he is transformed, or an ass's head before we say he is translated. It is this suddenness, the jump, the dark gap of apparent disconnection which moves us to wonder. Or do we just laugh? We deal in opposites, and the opposites can be either absurdly or magically disconnected, depending entirely on *our* point of view, not on the objects themselves.

Knowledge is the discovery of connections. Both science and art have this in common with nature: that the processes of all three are based on dissatisfaction with the present. Just as in nature this present form exists to be developed and converted into what is most suitable for the future, so scientific knowledge must also be a continuous process, a pursuit—a pursuit, the very word used by Franz Kafka to describe his writings, but 'pursuit' in the sense of 'hunt', of really and endlessly following a trail.

'Where is it leading?' asks Kafka. And he goes on:

It can (and this seems most likely) lead to madness. There's nothing more to be said about that. The pursuit goes through me and tears me apart. Or I can (can I?) manage to keep on my feet and thus let myself be carried along by the pursuit. Where do I get to then? The word 'pursuit' is only a metaphor. I can also say 'assault on the last earthly frontier', and indeed an assault from below, from mankind; and I can, since this too is only a metaphor, replace it by the metaphor of an assault from above, aimed at me from above.

Here, as so often in Kafka's writings, despair is wonderfully balanced by hope. The consolation of irrational fears is that they leave room for optimism, since we simply do not know. Philosophy defines our limitations, art expounds our possibilities. The evidence of our senses is the source of despair, but the writer allows himself to be carried along by the 'pursuit' because of an irrational expectation that there is a harmony which is actively assaulting him (in Kafka's phrase) from above. The alternative is madness, surrender to disconnection as a way of life—or of death. Either this or voluntary blindness.

The terror of the isolated moment bursts through in Kafka's

work, even when he is secretly hopeful. 'Somewhere help is waiting,' he says, 'and the beaters are driving me there.' But the terrible moment has to be experienced, for in this is the future, which can indeed be nowhere else. Soon after writing about the assault on the last earthly frontier Kafka noted in his diary: 'A moment of thought. Resign yourself, learn to rest in the moment. Yes, in the moment, the terrible moment. It is not terrible. Only the fear of the future makes it terrible.'

Creation is connection, and connection leads to creation, in man as in art. Only a day after his remark about the terrible moment which is not terrible, Kafka could see, in a possible child of his own, an image of perfection: 'The infinite, deep, warm, redeeming happiness of sitting beside the cradle of one's own child, opposite the mother.' And then, after a paragraph, he goes on: 'There is no evil. If you have crossed the threshold everything is good, and you must not speak.' Beyond morality, harmony eliminates contrasts and (specifically here) the contrasting tones of language.

Where does this leave the writer? Is language itself a perpetuation of that disharmony he hopes to transcend? It is a characteristic of so much writing in our time that it describes instead of presenting. Plays are tedious when they are no longer dramatic but epic, a constant circling of the object in paths of descriptive language. We are told about experience, instead of having experience presented in correlative forms. If you describe, you must reduce experience into forms which can be described; the language is there, and you cut phenomena to fit the language. In art it is the other way round. The phenomenon transforms language. Just as in nature, so in the language of art form evolves to suit the job in hand. Description is not an assault on the frontier but a tedious repetition inside the stockade. It denies the whole sense of pursuit, that dissatisfaction with the present which unites art and natural processes. Satisfaction with known language is a tribute to yesterday and is best left to encyclopedias.

But of course there is dissatisfaction. The experimenters, the architectural designers of language, from Joyce to the latest kinetic constructors, are looking for an expressive form which can adapt to the creative flow. Paul Klee says that the business of art is lending duration to genesis. By genesis he means a world in process of formation. The artist does not see nature as a completed image. How therefore can the completed artistic image be true? Is there a language which can fit the fluid process? When truth is a continuous process of growth, the only valid language must be as fluid and as transitory as the experience it presents. Is such a thing possible in human terms? Or must we, accepting the need for transformation, despair of language and even of art?

The writer will not be silenced. He has a hunger for speech, he wants to make sensible forms out of apparently senseless experience, he must probe that wordless mystery beyond organic perception, the silence which is both terrifying and tranquil. It is terrifying to reason but tranquil to faith. This is the coupling of Kafka's despair and glorious presumption. 'Somewhere help is waiting, and the beaters are driving me there.' Of course, all dissatisfaction with the present is blasphemous and revolutionary and necessary. Gottfried Benn describes life as 'a repetition of absurdities, an eternal residue of first steps paraded today as "history".' He goes on to claim that it is beyond history that reality begins. That is, beyond what we know and find absurdly incomplete.

If there is that ultimate silence of harmony, in which it is not necessary to speak, surely language, even the language of art, is an intrusion, a noise, a disturbance? How can art therefore lead to harmony? We are so conditioned by our concept of opposites that we accept too easily the proposition that noise is balanced by absence of noise, that silence means no sound. But is it not likely that ultimate silence is positive, a harmony of sound? The future is a transformation of the present, and in the present we are aware of the fragments but not of the whole, which is beyond immediate perception. That we are surrounded by fragments of noise is obvious—too obvious. Since nothing is lost, our present experience is amalgamated into the future, so if there is such a thing as ultimate silence it must contain what we now call sound.

Even in our present state of ignorance we can be aware that words depend on silence. The shape of words is invisible except against the background of silence. It is like the bird on the branch in a Japanese painting, a black shape isolated against white. In the plays of Chekhov we find patterns of words which could just as easily be called patterns of silence. Chekhov uses dialogue to cut silence into meaningful shapes. Here silence stands, in blocks, perceptible—and perceptibly engraved. Who can now tell which is the language—the words or the silence? It is futile to ask this question. We only ask it because we inflict opposites and sharp distinctions on ourselves. Language consists of words *and* silence, each helpless without the other. Words and silence interlock and are interdependent, a glimpse (as all true art is) of an ultimate harmony where silence is the ecstatic conjunction of language, the language of total perception.

The infinity of those vast spaces, once so terrifying, is made up of finite particles, and so is the language which shall disclose knowledge beyond our knowledge. The poet starts from the detail he knows. He develops a surface, conforming to natural pressures, responding to experience. This growth and ceaseless adaptation is as necessary to the language of art as to natural form. I doubt if a man can be a poet unless he is a scientist at heart, sharing that selfless obsession with the observed detail, the trivial, sacred fact which is the world to our perception, the only beginning of transformation. The poet is as interested as the scientist in the conservation of energy. In nature, in art, and in folk-tale, transformation is an acknowledgement that nothing is lost, nothing is irrelevant, one thing does lead to another until one thing becomes another.

Rilke wonders if the senses can ever coalesce. Only in this way, he thinks, through one all-embracing sense, can division be transcended. Experience, now divided and shared among our separate perceptions, would then be realized as total and one. Sound would be fused into a harmonious centre, since there could be no individual perception of noise. This is where Rilke places 'the unheard centre', the source of the song of Orpheus.

Gerard Manley Hopkins anticipates the idea of silence as ultimate sound in his early poem 'The Habit of Perfection', which begins:

> Elected Silence, sing to me
> And beat upon my whorlèd ear,
> Pipe me to pastures still and be
> The music that I care to hear.
>
> Shape nothing, lips; be lovely-dumb:
> It is the shut, the curfew sent
> From there where all surrenders come
> Which only makes you eloquent.

Is this perhaps the tranquillity of the wise, the natural silence, the arrival of the Tao condition where 'he who speaks does not know, he who knows does not speak'? Hopkins goes on to invoke the other senses, making it clear that the false division into sound and silence finds its parallel in these as well. If sound in silence seems contradictory, it is a contradiction imposed on us by our limited perceptions.

In Rilke's poetry Orpheus is both transformer and transformed. His music transforms apparent chaos into evident order, while he himself, as part of nature, is involved in the natural progression from one form to another. As transformer and transformed, Orpheus is no different from the smallest speck of matter. Each particle in nature is itself a product of change and a stage to future form. Is it surprising that each particle generates enormous meaning? Orpheus, like the particle, is not aware of divisions or fragments or oppositions; he is growth. The god is minute. Orpheus is a god and he represents the perfect poet in his song because he is entirely ordinary, a detail among details, surrendered to the habit of perfection—the most elusive state for mankind.

In the first of Rilke's Sonnets to Orpheus the music from that unheard centre, there where all surrenders come, creates (appropriately enough) what Rilke calls 'animals of silence'. The song of Orpheus is perfection. Therefore there are no separate strands of sound, but only their conjunction in the harmony of silence.

We know that the mythical Orpheus had power over animals. He had power over everything—trees, Jason's boat, the sea, men. His power, his magical potency, is the ordinary power of nature to establish connections. Before he exercises his power, the animals of the jungle are wild. Their cries are loud, insistent, and individual. This state represents our vision of the detached detail, the inexplicable extravagance of individual forms which seem in conflict with each other and with us.

When he tames the animals, Orpheus resolves the contradictions of that jungle which is man's experience. In this jungle is the tiger, traditionally the companion of Dionysus (the romantic principle) on his journey from the Oriental thickets. The roar of this animal is heard outside the defensive human stockade. This is chaos. The song of Orpheus is raised in the service of Apollo, the classical god of form. It unites the apparently disjointed details of our partial perception, those elements accepted by one sense (our sense of hearing) as individual sounds. When these are brought together in harmony, we reach the unheard centre. The animals of the jungle are suddenly mute. Their voices are conjoined in silence. They are indeed animals of silence.

These animals of silence are the reality beyond history. Kafka's 'pursuit', his assault on the last earthly frontier, is meant to carry him into the jungle which is no jungle at all but an expressive shape and an expressive silence. Here you must not speak.

A Note on Translations

The author is also the translator of the various quotations from German which appear in these essays.

Among available translations of the main German works mentioned are the following:

J. W. VON GOETHE (1749–1832)

Faust Parts I and II, trans. P. Wayne (1949, 1959)

The Sufferings of Young Werther (Die Leiden des jungen Werthers), trans. B. Q. Morgan (1966)

Elective Affinities (Die Wahlverwandtschaften), trans. R. J. Hollingdale (1971)

Selected Verse, with prose translations by F. David Luke (1964)

GEORG BÜCHNER (1813–1837)

The Plays of Georg Büchner, trans. Victor Price (1971)

HUGO VON HOFMANNSTHAL (1874–1929)

'The Letter of Lord Chandos' ('Ein Brief'), in *Selected Prose*, trans. M. Hottinger, Tania and James Stern (1952)

RAINER MARIA RILKE (1875–1926)

'Primal Sound' ('Ur-Geräusch'), in *Selected Works*, vol. I: Prose, trans. G. Craig Houston (1954)

'Duino Elegies', 'Sonnets to Orpheus', and other poems in *Selected Works*, vol. II: Poetry, trans. J. B. Leishman (1960)

The Notebook of Malte Laurids Brigge (Die Aufzeichnungen des Malte Laurids Brigge), trans. John Linton (1959)

HERMANN HESSE (1877–1962)

Steppenwolf (Der Steppenwolf), trans. B. Creighton, rev. by W. Sorrell (1969)

The Glass Bead Game (Das Glasperlenspiel), trans. Richard and Clara Winston (1970)

ROBERT MUSIL (1880–1942)

Young Törless (Die Verwirrungen des Zöglings Törless), trans. Eithne Wilkins and Ernst Kaiser (1955)

FRANZ KAFKA (1883–1924)

The Trial (Der Prozess), trans. Willa and Edwin Muir (1953)

'Metamorphosis' ('Die Verwandlung'), in *Metamorphosis and Other Stories*, trans. Willa and Edwin Muir (1970)

Diaries 1910–1923 (Tagebücher), ed. Max Brod, trans. Joseph Kresh (1964)

Conversations with Kafka (Gesprache mit Kafka) by Gustav Janouch, trans. Goronwy Rees (1971)